# REDEFINE WEALTH FOR YOURSELF

### How to Stop Chasing Money and Finally Live Your Life's Purpose

SEEK WISDOM,

Patrice Washington

Redefine Wealth for Yourself: How to Stop Chasing Money and Finally Live Your Life's Purpose

Published by Seek Wisdom Find Wealth Publishing
Atlanta, GA
www.PatriceWashington.com

Distributed by Seek Wisdom Find Wealth Publishing

For ordering information or special discounts for bulk purchases, please contact Seek Wisdom Find Wealth at 11770 Haynes Bridge Rd. #205-493, Alpharetta, GA 30009 or e-mail info@seekwisdomfindwealth.com.

Cover Design by Brand Quality
Cover Photo by Priiincesss
Interior Design by JERA Publishing

Paperback ISBN: 978-0-9859080-6-5
Hardcover ISBN: 978-0-9859080-9-6

First Edition

*To Purpose Chasers all over the world*
*Your commitment to Redefining Wealth inspires me to*
*wake up every day and chase purpose—not money.*

# Contents

# The Truth about Wealth

I NEVER SAW MY financial demise coming.

In 2007, when I was twenty weeks pregnant, I took a bad fall down the stairs. A year earlier, we had lost a son, born at twenty-four weeks. He weighed a pound and a half and lived just five hours before he passed away in my arms, and I prayed this pregnancy would have a different outcome. I checked in to the hospital, where I followed my doctor's orders for bed rest.

While my family was in jeopardy, I found some solace in my financial security. I had health insurance, and the real estate business I'd started while still in college had grown into a seven-figure empire. We were bringing in six figures a month, and because I was doing what I believed were all the right things, I expected the good times to keep rolling. My expectations were wrong.

Soon after my hospital stay began, news reports about the real estate industry and the economy both turned dire and pessimistic. The real estate bubble, they said, was starting to burst, and the ramifications would affect us all. I had sixteen team members on payroll, and they increasingly called me throughout the day to tell me about deals falling through and clients failing to get loan approval. They didn't know what was happening or what to do about it, and I had no idea what to tell them.

1

Every day, the reports got worse. I watched news shows as if I would learn some new fact that would change everything. In reality, it wouldn't have mattered if I'd been in the office every day because there was very little I could do. Still, I consumed all the news about the economic downturn until about five weeks into my stay, when my doctor looked at the readout on the baby's monitor and frowned at me. "If you don't stop stressing out," she said, "you're going to leave here two years in a row with no baby."

It was clear my financial reality would be irrevocably changed by the time I left the hospital, so in the interest of my daughter's health, I made a decision to surrender. I had the TV removed from my room and tried to focus only on what I could control. Five weeks later, at thirty weeks, our daughter, Reagan, came into the world. Healthy and strong, but still premature, she spent the next three weeks in the neonatal intensive care unit.

Turning off my television reduced my stress, but it did nothing to change the reality of the economy. In the following weeks and months, banks went out of business and mortgage companies shut their doors. Homeowners went from feeling secure in their homes to underwater on their mortgages. Around the country, as foreclosure rates skyrocketed, many people looked at the numbers and walked away from their homes.

We were taking financial hits from every direction. Our insurance company canceled my coverage, and we left the hospital with $400,000 in medical bills. We owned thirteen rental properties, but one by one, the tenants stopped paying rent, and given that they were out of work, there wasn't much we could do to collect. For the next year, my husband, Gerald, and I tried everything we could think of to save our business, but by then, there was nothing left to save. We surrendered our luxury SUVs and moved from our six-thousand-square-foot home in Los Angeles, where we'd both grown up, to a six-hundred-square-foot apartment in Metairie, Louisiana, where we had a property we'd hoped to flip until a contractor ripped us off.

One day, while Gerald and Reagan were out, I shut myself in the tiny bathroom, where I often went to be alone to think and pray. I couldn't understand how, after trying to do everything right, I'd ended up losing it all. "Why me, God?" I asked. "What did I do wrong?" My conversation with God became a bawling, snorting, ugly cry, and I fell to my knees on the bathroom floor. My head pressed to the linoleum, I wept and called out, "God, what am I going to do?"

In that moment, I heard that small voice telling me to turn to my Bible, where I landed on Proverbs 17:16. To paraphrase, it read: "What good is money in the hands of a fool if they have no desire to seek wisdom?" That moment was the beginning of climbing out of my dark valley. I decided I would get wise counsel. I would seek wisdom—not just knowledge—in order to find wealth. I also committed to sharing whatever I learned along the way with anyone willing to listen.

I took the passion for financial education I'd developed while running my real estate business and used it to start over. I published an ugly little blog, where I shared my journey and the changes I was making in my life. As a speaker, and then as an author and coach, I built a new business, and I recovered financially. That moment on the bathroom floor changed everything. I'm in a much better position today than I was in when the real estate bubble burst.

None of my financial recovery happened overnight. *In Redefining Wealth for Yourself,* I share with you the steps I took to create a solid financial foundation for myself and my family. I also share what I discovered through my struggles in other areas of my life, all of which affected my ability to attract wealth.

Over those years, I've struggled to create harmony between work and home. I've gone to therapy to work on my marriage and to stay sharp and perform at my best. I've discovered how real the seven-year itch is and faced the possibility of losing my marriage before doing the work to rebuild our relationship. I've pushed myself hard when my body needed rest and nourishment, and I've found myself doing the right work in the wrong place. Through it all, I've witnessed firsthand that money is only a small fraction of what makes for a truly wealthy life.

I wrote *Redefining Wealth for Yourself* to share with you the habits, tools, and routines I've used to create a wealthy life as I define it. Define wealth for yourself, but never feel guilty about desiring more money.

Money is a tool that opens doors and solves problems. Our economy runs on money, and there's nothing wrong with wanting to enjoy the finer things in life. I do! My purpose here is to help you understand how you can live your life's purpose, find fulfillment, and earn more than you've ever imagined without chasing money.

## THE SIX PILLARS OF WEALTH

The twelfth-century definition of wealth is the condition of wellbeing or happiness. Money is only one factor in that happiness. When you take care of those things that make life worthwhile, you become the kind of person who attracts and receives the wealth you desire. Money is a result of understanding what you want and who you have to become to actually receive it.

The sections of *Redefining Wealth for Yourself* are based on the Six Pillars of Wealth:

1. FIT: Become your best self.
2. PEOPLE: Take care of relationships that matter.
3. SPACE: Set up your life to support you.
4. FAITH: Believe in something greater.
5. WORK: Live your life's purpose.
6. MONEY: Attract the prosperity you desire.

I take a holistic approach to wealth because these aspects of your life are inextricably linked. They all affect your ability to attract prosperity. Mastering these things, some of which may seem to have nothing to do with money, will create a positive ripple effect that will touch and impact every aspect of your life. Our culture teaches us to strive first for money and material success, but without a strong foundation in the other pillars, all that striving will be for nothing. You'll either struggle to sustain your material wealth or you'll be too unhealthy and unhappy to enjoy it.

# HOW TO USE THIS BOOK

If you're tempted to flip forward and jump into the Work pillar or the Money pillar, stop and assess your performance in each other pillar first. If you can give yourself a ten out of ten in your physical and mental fitness, your mindset, your personal and professional relationships, the energy and organization of the spaces where you live and work, and your faith practices, then by all means, jump ahead. You've either been doing this work for a while or you're superhuman. However, if you'd give yourself less than a perfect score in any of the first four pillars, slow down and do the work in order. Don't skip steps. Choose to chase your purpose instead. Choose to start with the pillars in the order in which I've laid them out. Dedicate a journal to your Redefining Wealth journey and take action on the exercises at the end of each chapter.

Building wealth and creating a wealthy life is a marathon, not a sprint. Don't expect yourself to make these changes overnight. Don't expect perfection. Commit to applying these principles, taking on new habits, and paying attention to how your life changes in the process. Get support, accountability, and inspiration, in the free Purpose Chasers community. Join us at iamapurposechaser.com. I'd love to see you share your wins in our group.

Let's get started on your journey to redefining wealth for yourself and achieving your wealthy life!

# PART I. FIT

## Become Your Best Self

A WEALTHY LIFE—A LIFE of sustained wellbeing—requires a strong foundation of physical, mental, and emotional fitness. This kind of wealth can only happen with a radical commitment to intentionally changing the areas of your life that are not in alignment with what you envision for your future. It requires you to become the strongest, healthiest version of yourself so you can sustain and enjoy everything you build.

If you ignore your physical health while you chase money, you might fill your bank account, but you'll suffer along the way. If you neglect your mental and emotional wellbeing now, you'll make the journey much harder than it has to be, and in the end, you won't reach your desired destination. The simple, yet powerful strategies in this section will help you level up your physical health and fitness, develop mindsets of confidence and abundance, and address emotional trauma and mental illness. You cannot have wealth without health. Get your FIT pillar all the way together with these principles, and you'll position yourself for success with all the other pillars.

**CHAPTER 1**

# Protect the Vessel

A T THIRTY-FOUR YEARS old, I had trouble climbing four flights of stairs to go from the parking garage to my bedroom in our townhome. By the time I reached the third story on any given day, I wanted to sit and catch my breath. Even though I didn't appear to be out of shape or overweight, my apparent lack of fitness convinced me I needed to work out more.

In my workout class, I couldn't keep up with the other women, most of whom were at least ten years older than I was. I struggled through my workouts until, one day, I happened to find myself in the emergency room with a case of food poisoning. The doctor tested my blood and discovered the real issue. I wasn't out of shape. My hemoglobin level was less than half what it should've been. My body was low on both blood and iron.

"If you were in an accident with the levels you have now," the doctor explained, "you'd have a good chance of quickly bleeding to death." Around the same time, I was struggling with fertility issues, and the doctor explained I couldn't carry a baby with my blood levels. "You don't have enough blood to share with a baby," he said.

Neither my struggle to breathe nor my difficulty conceiving had driven me to the doctor. I was too busy, I'd told myself, to be running back and forth to medical appointments. Instead, I self-diagnosed, like many busy, professional women I know, and I got it completely wrong. My body was crying out for an iron infusion. If I'd pushed myself much more, I would've needed a full-blown blood transfusion.

During this time, I was bringing to life a big vision. HarperCollins had picked up my second book, *Real Money Answers for Every Woman*, a few years after I self-published it. I was gearing up for a national book tour and praying for God to enlarge my territory, but I was running my body into the ground. I was so focused on my goals that I failed to protect the vessel I needed to achieve them. My prayer to be an internationally recognized author and speaker didn't come to fruition until I took my health seriously and prepared for the demands that came along with the dream.

You can pray every day for God to open doors and make your vision a reality, but you must also be prepared to have the physical endurance required to live that vision. As your physical wellbeing improves, your ability to execute your vision grows. With that in mind, ask yourself every day what you can do to get ready to walk into your vision. If God gave you exactly what you're asking for today, right this moment, would you be ready for it? Could you handle the physical demands? Do you have the stamina? If your answer to any of those questions is no, then you have work to do. Get clear about your vision and commit to becoming your best self so you can bring your vision to fruition. To redefine wealth for yourself and create it in your own life, you must protect the vessel.

## 1. COMMIT TO YOUR OWN PROCESS

In my online community, a woman shared a fitness goal of walking ten thousand steps a day, and within minutes another woman responded, "Well, I can't do ten thousand steps. I can only do five or six thousand." Rather than focus on her own ability and goals, she immediately went into comparison and found herself lacking. These women didn't know each other at all. The second woman knew nothing about the first, yet she felt like she was somehow in competition with her.

When you commit to your own process and set goals specific to where you are now and where you want to be, you don't have to compete against anyone else. When you're not in comparison, you become more courageous. You no longer worry about judgment from the people to whom you might ordinarily compare yourself. Your fitness goals are only determined by you, your current fitness level and what you want to achieve.

When I heard myself say, for what must've been the millionth time, "What you verbalize you magnetize," I realized three small words—*I don't run*—had negatively impacted my life for twenty years. I looked at my daughter and the way she runs all over the house. It comes naturally to her, as it does to most kids, as it did to me when I was a kid. I never pinpointed exactly when or why I decided I wasn't a runner, but that thought—*I don't run*— kept me from being my best possible self for two decades of my life.

Finally, I asked myself, "Why do you keep saying that? You're pretty healthy. You have fully functioning knees and feet. You can run." I stopped comparing myself to other runners, and I started running. In the beginning, it took me seventeen or eighteen minutes to do a mile. Within a year, I got my mile down to about twelve minutes because I committed to my own process without worrying about what anyone else was doing. My goal was to do better than my initial time, and I've since become a regular runner.

Rather than worry about how fast or strong or fit everyone else is, compete instead against who you were yesterday. Whether you're in the gym or out for a walk, focus on your progress. Be more committed to yourself, to your goals, and to protecting the vessel you need to execute the vision than you are to keeping up with other people. Commit to your own process and let them worry about theirs.

### Redefine Wealth for Yourself

Choose your most important health or fitness goal and define a series of action steps or behavioral changes that will help you achieve it. Regardless of what your friend or colleague is doing, make sure the steps you spell out suit you.

## 2. LISTEN TO YOUR BODY

At the height of the juice craze, I drank a twenty-four-ounce juice for breakfast every morning, but during that time, I kept getting sick. My body was telling me something was wrong, so I saw a doctor, who gave me pills to treat my symptoms. She advised me to either expect to take those pills for the rest of my life or see a nutritionist to get to the root of the problem.

I kept a food journal for a couple of weeks, and when I met with the naturopathic nutritionist, she explained the fruit-based juices caused my blood sugar to spike every morning. All the fruit sugar was also feeding a candida overgrowth in my body. Even though I ate plenty of veggies, it wasn't enough to balance the sugar I was putting directly in my bloodstream. Fruit juices, in large quantities, didn't serve my body well.

Based on her recommendations, I cut out fruits, bread, and high-sugar vegetables for about six months. The change required discipline, but it didn't take long for me to feel better, and I stopped getting sick. Because of the changes I'd made for the sake of my health, I had more focus throughout the work day, I experienced greater clarity, since the brain fog I didn't even realize I was experiencing faded away, and I lost eighteen pounds of excess body fat.

A few months into my new protocol, I got my first call to do a nationally syndicated television show. At that point, I felt better, so I performed at my highest level. My appearance went well, and the producers invited me back. In many ways, the discipline required to become my best self had set me up to walk into my destiny.

Low energy, skin issues, difficulty sleeping, persistent injuries, and frequent illnesses are your body's ways of telling you something needs to change. Everybody's different and every *body* is different. Be proactive and figure out what works for you in your diet and exercise routine. Listen to your body. When your face or your belly is bloated, that's a sign. When you wake up exhausted after sleeping seven or eight hours, that's a sign. When you have any recurring symptoms, what you're putting in your body is likely a factor, but you may need to see a healthcare practitioner to figure out what's really going on.

Be willing to make changes even if they feel like sacrifices. Your body will tell you when you're on the right track with your eating choices and your physical activity. Glowing skin, high energy, restful sleep, a healthy weight, clear thinking—these are all symptoms of healthy choices.

> ### Redefine Wealth for Yourself
> For one week, write down everything you eat and how you feel throughout the day. Note your energy level, quality of sleep, and anything troubling, such as headaches, bloating, or upset stomach after meals. Choose to eliminate foods that don't serve you well or contact a nutritionist who can help you make better food choices.

## 3. SCHEDULE THE APPOINTMENT

Two and a half years had passed since my husband last saw the dentist. Over and over, he canceled the appointments or no-showed. Something else was always more important—until his temporary crown cracked, leaving a nerve exposed. The pain was so bad it sent him to a random dentist to have a root canal in the middle of the night. The emergency service was inconvenient and cost $1500 more than a regular appointment.

For my husband, the cost of putting off his health care was temporary pain and extra money. For some people, however, the price is much higher. It's a blood sugar issue that could've been reversed before it became diabetes. It's a heart attack that could've been prevented or a stage IV cancer diagnosis that could have been caught in the earlier.

Staying on top of your doctor's visits, can save you a lot of pain. It can save your life, and even when the issues are less serious, it can save you money on prescriptions and procedures you can avoid with regular checkups. Preventative care is so much more affordable and effective and so much less painful than reactive care.

In a society that values busyness, and especially as women juggling the responsibilities of work and family, we often get so caught up in hustling, grinding, and taking care of everyone else that we barely cover the basics of maintaining our own health. That has to stop. Have an annual checkup. See your dentist every six months. Based on your age and medical history, you may need to have a mammogram, colonoscopy, or other testing on a regular basis. Schedule those appointments and keep them. If you're in pain or you've been dealing with an issue for a long time, find a specialist in your area and make an appointment today. Your life may depend on it. Your quality of life and ability fulfill your purpose certainly do.

### Redefine Wealth for Yourself

If you're not on a regular schedule for physicals and dental exams, take out your phone and make those appointments. Ask your general practitioner what other medical appointments are appropriate for your age and health history, and make them right away.

## 4. MAKE TIME TO MOVE DAILY

Most of us sit in front of a computer all day, so making time to consistently move your body requires commitment and planning. Brandi Harvey, author of *Breakthrough Sold Separately* and founder of BeyondHer. co, an active wellness destination, knows what it takes to create an exercise habit. These days, she regularly works out at her favorite local gym, but she wasn't always into fitness.

Having suffered from allergies and asthma as a child, Brandi developed the habit of staying indoors and living a rather sedentary life. That all changed when she was nineteen-years-old, and her father, comedian Steve Harvey, took one look at Brandi and her twin sister, Karli, and described the girls as "fluffy." While it was more of an observation than a criticism, the word lit a fire in Brandi. She started working out for the first time and eventually became a fitness instructor and a fitness competitor.

In her *Redefining Wealth* podcast interview, I talked with Brandi about what it takes to make exercise a regular part of your life. "Greatness never goes on sale," she said. "You have to pay full price." You define greatness for yourself, of course, just like you define your idea of wealth. As with every aspect of wealth, the price you'll pay for greatness in your physical fitness is one of time, consistency, and lifelong commitment. It may feel like you don't have time for exercise, but you must decide it's important enough to do no matter what. You cannot build this FIT pillar without developing your physical fitness.

Regular exercise can help you achieve the following health goals:

- Increase cardiovascular fitness.
- Build and maintain muscle and bone mass.
- Sleep better.
- Reduce depression and anxiety.
- Achieve and maintain a healthy weight.
- Have more energy.
- Improve your mood.
- Manage stress in a healthy way.
- Reach and maintain healthy cholesterol levels.
- Improve your blood pressure numbers.
- Reduce your risks of certain cancers.
- Decrease your risk of diabetes and improve blood sugar levels.
- Avoid or improve sleep apnea.
- Enhance your sex life.

A walk on a nearby trail or around your neighborhood, taking the stairs several times each day, walking the hallways in your office building on your lunch break—these micro-activities add up. You don't have to go hard at the gym every day. Find a routine that works for you. Make time to move daily and enjoy a combination of benefits you can only get from regular physical activity.

*Redefine Wealth for Yourself*
If you already have a consistent workout routine, great. Stick with it. If not talk to your doctor about any relevant health concerns, and then start small. Commit to a certain number of minutes or steps each day. Over time, experiment and find the kinds of exercise that work best for you.

# 5. GO THE HECK TO SLEEP

Night after night, my daughter, Reagan, dozed off while completing her homework. Her fourth-grade workload was intense, but when I suggested she take a bath and a nap and then get back to the work, she refused. "I have to finish my work before I go to sleep," she insisted. I explained to Reagan what I want you to know. You cannot do your best work when you're tired.

When you're well rested, your focus improves, you can work faster, and you can do a better job. On the surface, it seems noble to sacrifice rest for work, but that mindset can lead to unnecessary errors. Unfortunately, the idea of shortchanging sleep has become a part of our culture of achievement.

#teamnosleep
*Sleep is for suckers.*
*I'll sleep when I'm dead.*
*Rich people don't sleep eight hours a day.*

The people behind those messages want you to believe you need to work around the clock to achieve your goals, but it's not true. In fact, the average person needs about eight hours of sleep every night for the body and brain to function at optimal levels. Once in a while, you might have to sacrifice some sleep in pursuit of your dreams, but that can't be an ongoing practice. You can't skimp on sleep for weeks, months, and years on end without suffering negative consequences.

A lack of quality sleep is linked to serious health issues. It can increase your risk of obesity, depression, diabetes, heart disease, and some types of cancer. It makes it hard for you to lose weight and build muscle. A lack of sleep can even put you at greater risk of one day developing Alzheimer's disease. It lowers your immune system so you get sick more often, and drowsy driving significantly increases your risk of accidents.

If you're like most people, you're easier to get along with when you're well rested. You make better decisions and you experience less anxiety. You manage stress better. You're more creative and more productive. So much for skipping sleep so you can achieve success more quickly. It just doesn't work. In fact, for many people, sufficient sleep is the missing element preventing you from bringing your vision to life. It's that serious. Protect your vessel. Please, get some sleep.

### Redefine Wealth for Yourself

Set a bedtime that allows you to get sufficient sleep and stick to it. If you have trouble falling asleep or find yourself waking up too early or too often, don't give up. Simple lifestyle changes can eliminate obstacles to sleep. Check out one of my favorite resources on this subject, *Sleep Smarter* by Shawn Stevenson, or talk to your healthcare professional about natural ways to sleep better.

## 6. MEAL PREP WEEKLY

One of my strengths is my ability to focus and not get distracted, but sometimes I focus so much on my work that I sit at my desk all day without eating anything. The day flies by, and I skip lunch completely. This isn't a productive habit. Not eating enough is the nutritional equivalent of surviving on junk food. When I did this often, I messed up my metabolism and taught my body to hoard fuel by storing fat. I was hitting the gym, but I wasn't seeing the progress I wanted because I wasn't giving my body the nutrition it needed.

I barely ate twice a day, so when I participated in a challenge at the gym that suggested we eat every three hours, it was a real stretch for me. I was only able to stick to the meal plan because my husband, Gerald, and I meal prepped for the week on Sundays. It worked so well for us that it became a habit. On most Sunday afternoons, we prepare our meals for the week. Sometimes, one of us has to do it without the other, but when we do it together, it's a great bonding activity, and we eat well for the rest of the week.

By investing a few hours on Sunday afternoon, we save all the time we'd usually spend during the week figuring out what we're going to eat, what to cook, or what to pick up. It's already done. We save money because we don't feel tempted to eat out. And we save our health because we choose to prep foods that nourish and energize us.

Prepping your meals in advance allows you to be intentional about what you put into your body. This includes having healthy snacks to go so you never have to buy a bag of chips at the gas station. When your meals are already made, you stop skipping meals and stop training your body to cling desperately to its fat stores. You stop making bad food decisions because you never have to get overly hungry. With meal prepping, the decision to eat well is already made.

You always have the option of using meal-prepping services, which deliver prepared meals or all the ingredients you need to prepare them. Ultimately, it doesn't matter if you do it yourself or pay someone else to do it. Meal prepping for the week is still one of the most effective ways you can take care of you FIT pillar.

### Redefine Wealth for Yourself

Decide if you need a service or will meal prep for yourself. If you go with a service, do some research and test different options. To prep your own meals, pick a day and time when you'll shop for the ingredients and when you'll prep. For ideas, search online for meal-prep plans and choose one to implement.

## 7. GET OFF WELLBEING WELFARE

The results from my workouts were worth the effort, but my muscles were constantly sore. Since getting a massage several times a week wasn't practical, I joined a nearby urban sweat lodge, where I was wrapped in a warm, fragrant cocoon and left to relax. No phone. No laptop. No family demands. The treatment soothed my sore muscles and gave me space to unplug from the day. It was affordable and accessible and easily fit my schedule. Self-care was high on my priority list, so I enjoyed the sweat lodge regularly.

Prioritizing self-care requires you to prioritize yourself. It requires you to ditch wellbeing welfare, a concept Mikki Taylor, beauty authority and author of *Editor-in-Chic*, introduced me to when I interviewed her on my podcast. Wellbeing welfare is the belief that you only deserve to treat yourself or your body well on special occasions, usually when someone else gives you a gift certificate for the local spa.

With wellbeing welfare, you depend on other people to give you permission to take care of you, but when you ditch this mentality, you decide when and how you'll take care of yourself. Owning your self-care starts with reframing the way you see it, so begin to think of self-care as a need you should meet every day. Keep in mind also self-care doesn't have to cost a lot of money or time.

Mikki Taylor says, "You have the choice to treat your body like a temple or like a trailer park." You enter a temple with awe and reverence. You speak in hushed tones and handle objects with great care. You admire every element. Imagine treating your body, the physical manifestation of yourself, with the same reverence. It changes how you show up in the world. It changes how the world responds to you.

Waiting on welfare, on the other hand, teaches people you're willing to settle for leftovers. Stop waiting. Claim your wellbeing for yourself. Look at what makes you happy, helps you relax, and allows you to replenish. Schedule a regular massage or have a facial. Go to a spa once a quarter or on a silent retreat once a year. Sometimes, self-care can be as simple as spending time alone. It can be as easy as taking yourself out to lunch after church every Sunday, going to a local museum by yourself, or taking a nap in your favorite pajamas.

You deserve more than just getting your nails done every few weeks. You deserve the massage, the body polish, the colonic, the facial, and your time in the infrared sauna. If a particular treatment or experience helps you function at a higher level because it leaves you feeling rested, at peace, and comfortable in your body, it deserves a place in your budget. Invest in your self-care at a level that makes sense for you. Make room in your budget and your calendar for whatever leaves you feeling replenished. You deserve more than wellbeing welfare.

### Redefine Wealth for Yourself

Examine your calendar and your budget to find room for your favorite self-care practices. Set aside the time and money to enjoy the treatments or experiences that nurture your body, mind, and spirit.

## CHAPTER 2

# Develop a Fit Mindset

WHEN I WROTE my second book, *Real Money Answers for Every Woman*, I spent a lot of time in my local Starbucks. One day, a man at a nearby table told me he was also writing a book. Weeks later, I finished my book and sent it off to be published, and when I decided to write my next book, I started going to Starbucks again. A year had passed, but when the same man came in, we recognized each other. I was typing away on my keyboard. "Oh," he said, "so you're still working on your book."

"No, that one's already out," I explained. "I'm writing the next one now." *Real Money Answers for Men* was my third in the series. Before I could ask him how his book had turned out, the gentleman informed me he hadn't finished it yet, and he launched into all the reasons why. Bottom line: he'd spent three years working on the same project and still had nothing to show for it.

I had a purpose as an author. I wanted my books to reach as many people as possible. I wanted to become a bestselling author several times over. I wanted to create a legacy. I was confident about the value I had to offer my readers, and nothing would stand in the way of achieving my publishing goals. I had a family to take care of and other work to do, but I couldn't allow excuses, naysayers or a fear of failure to keep me from executing my vision.

I have no idea if my colleague from Starbucks ever published his book. I hope he did, but if not, he's not unusual. People often tell me they want to write a book, save more money, launch a business, find a better job, or finally get physically fit. However, many of those people never take significant, consistent action, and they never come close to achieving their dreams.

Creating a wealthy life requires you to take actions, day after day, for years. Just like you need a healthy body and mind for this journey, you also need to get your mindset in shape to do the required work. Every change in your life starts with a shift in mindset, a new way of thinking that allows you to make better decisions and see your goals through to completion. Becoming wealthy is no different.

Your mindset—what you believe is true about you, the world, and what's possible—will determine whether or not you ever achieve your goals. Building wealth of any kind requires mental fortitude because the journey is filled with ups and downs and twists and turns. You have to prepare your mind to weather it all. If not, you may get worn down and give up before you experience the fruits of your efforts. When you have a fit mindset, you know who you are and you know how to handle the slings and arrows life will inevitably throw your way.

## 8. CREATE A DAILY MANTRA

My husband and I lost all our material wealth—our money, cars, home, real estate investments, and business assets—early in the Great Recession. With our properties gone, our businesses defunct, and our matching Range Rovers turned in to the dealer, we had to make some tough decisions. We still had a yellow cargo van we owned outright. The vehicle had a hole in the floor, was covered in residue from old marketing stickers, and had expired tags. If you've ever ridden in a cargo van, you know two things. One, they're drafty, and two, they only have two seats. Not only were we cold, but our infant daughter rode in her car seat on the floor of the van because there was no seat to buckle her in. (Dangerous, I know!)

The van could have become our new normal, but Gerald and I were in agreement. Financial struggle wouldn't be our reality forever. We needed the right mindset to keep us going when things looked bleakest. To nurture a fit mindset, we created daily mantras to program ourselves for success. When we drove past beautiful homes or passed a Range Rover, instead of going into a "woe is me" story, we said out loud: "Been there, done that, on the way back."

Our mantra reminded us of what was possible and evidence showed up to confirm our belief. In fact, the first car I purchased after moving to Atlanta was an older model Ranger Rover, which I paid for by bartering with the owner to do some work as the office manager of her salon. There would've been nothing wrong with shopping for a more modest car, but driving the Range Rover reminded me I was on my way back up. It was a tangible manifestation of the truth behind our mantra.

Even though we never shared our mantra with anyone else, so many people worked with us to help us recover. Because we kept "Been there, done that, on the way back" top of mind, we were able to spot unconventional opportunities to earn money during a time when this country's unemployment rate was abysmal. These days, we're no longer on the way back. We're in a much better position than we were before the recession. We made that mantra our reality.

Words are powerful, and a mantra isn't some woo-woo manifestation hocus-pocus. The repetition of a daily mantra reprograms your brain to expect more of what you tell it to expect. Scientists estimate your brain produces 70,000 thoughts per day. If you spend ten or fifteen minutes monitoring those thoughts, you might be surprised by how negative some of them can be. However, you have the ability to choose thoughts that serve you, and your mantra can help you do that.

The world has already programmed your thoughts. Many of the consistent messages you got from your parents, teachers, church leaders, and society in your childhood and adolescence are wired into your brain through neural connections. Because of cognitive bias, humans tend to believe what the people closest to us believe even in adulthood. Cognitive bias also causes the brain to seek evidence to prove what it already believes and ignore anything that contradicts those old beliefs. So if your fourth-grade teacher said you'd never amount to anything and you believed it, your brain might spend a lifetime proving it to be true. In that case, you'll likely struggle to see or take advantage of opportunities to prove the belief wrong.

Fortunately, you have neuroplasticity on your side. You can create new neural connections in your brain based on beliefs that serve you. It requires consistency and repetition to override those old beliefs and create new ones, but it's possible when you're intentional about choosing the thoughts you think. Practice a daily mantra to stay focused on your goals and to replace or respond to negative self-talk with something positive.

When your brain says you can't, tell it why you can. Use your daily mantra to talk to yourself and convince yourself of what's possible for you. You might find your daily mantra in your own experience, a Bible verse, an inspirational quote, or an affirmation. It doesn't matter where it comes from or who said it. What matters is that it serves to program your brain for success.

### Redefine Wealth for Yourself

Create your personal mantra. Make sure the statement moves you in a positive direction and resonates with you. Write a short, to-the-point statement like ours or draft something a little longer. Post your mantra where you'll see it or set reminders so it pops up on your phone. Develop a habit of saying it out loud to yourself. What you verbalize, you magnify and magnetize in your life.

## 9. WRITE YOUR STANDARDS

My second-grade teacher, Mrs. Parker, loved me dearly. She saw me as a gifted child and wanted me to make the most of my giftedness, but she had one problem with me. I talked way too much. While I now recognize talking as one of my gifts, Mrs. Parker was trying to manage her classroom. I thought I was being helpful by telling my friends and classmates how to do the work I'd already finished. I loved talking and I loved helping people, so it was a losing battle for my teacher.

Mrs. Parker never gave up on her mission to get me to close my mouth in class. She required me to write standards like "I will not talk in class" over and over, but the punishment turned out to be a gift. Later in my life, writing my standards in my journal became a tool to shift my mindset to manifest what I want. The practice didn't make me talk any less (because I didn't want to), but today it helps me convince myself of what I can achieve.

During my sophomore year in college, I worked hard to be admitted to the business school, and things were going well until I got to a weed-out math class. It was incredibly competitive, and I was close to failing. However, I'd gotten really into journaling around that time, and I started to write my standards for my math class: "I will get an A on the next quiz" and "I will get a B in this class." I wrote each standard in my thirty, forty, or fifty times each day, and I began to believe I could possibly pass. The writing process calmed my brain and reduced my anxiety, and I started to take action in the direction of my goal. It's a practice I still use regularly.

I didn't know it as a college student, but I was tapping into the power of neuroplasticity. I was shutting down thoughts of failure and rewiring my brain to believe I could, in fact, do well and earn the grade I needed. My brain started to look for ways I could succeed, and while I didn't get a B, I did get a B-. Had I not passed that class, I wouldn't have gotten into the business school, and had I not gotten into business school, I wouldn't be pursuing my MBA. My career would likely have taken a completely different path. I've used the process of writing my standards in the pursuit of a new job and when we were shopping for a new home. I got that job, and we live in that house today.

When you have big goals, you have to stay focused on your intention, and writing your standards by hand helps you do that. Handwriting taps into the learning centers in the brain and helps you retain information. Your motor skills and memory are engaged, and your brain registers what you're writing as important and filters out other information. This makes writing your standards by hand an ideal tool to help you develop a fit mindset. Just remember the act of writing doesn't make your goals come true. Instead, it helps you strengthen your belief in what you can accomplish so you can take action to make it happen.

### Redefine Wealth for Yourself

Grab a notebook, journal, or sheet of paper. Choose a new standard you're setting for yourself in any area of life and sum it up in one sentence. Write the sentence thirty, forty, or a hundred times. Be open to seeing the words on the page as true and make writing your standards a regular practice.

## 10. SAY IT IN THE MIRROR

In my early twenties, when Gerald and I were dating, I came home from a twenty-one-day trip to Spain and Italy to find he'd completely furnished my new apartment. It was a wonderful, thoughtful surprise. I looked around the room and took it all in. And then I quickly fled the apartment in tears.

Gerald was, to state the obvious, shocked and confused. When I was able to speak, I asked him, "Why would you put all those pictures up in there?" He'd decorated my place with huge posters of magazine covers, like *Essence*, *Sports Illustrated*, and *Black Enterprise*, with me as the cover model.

"I love those pictures of you," Gerald explained.

"But they're so ugly." I explained that I didn't like seeing myself. In fact, I only looked in the mirror when I had to, and when I did, I saw a girl who got the short end of the stick in every way—my hair, my skin, my lips. I was confident in my intelligence, my personality, and my ability to make money. But I'd spent my childhood hearing how ugly I was, and because the message often came from people close to me, I believed it.

That night, Gerald stood in front of the bathroom mirror with me and described everything he found beautiful about me, but I couldn't take it in. I still made him take all the pictures down. Later, my first therapist assigned me a similar exercise. I stood in front of the mirror and affirmed the young woman reflected back at me. Over time, as I found nice things to say about my appearance, my perspective shifted a little at a time. It wasn't easy, but I could accept compliments about my looks and actually believe them. Eventually, I saw my own beauty. I also developed a new compassion for myself. It was life-changing work for me.

Even though I've long since moved beyond that particular issue, talking to myself while looking in my own eyes still allows me to connect with myself. Before I go onstage or on set, I take my last bathroom break to talk to myself in the mirror. I affirm: "You deserve to be here. You are here for a reason. You have a word for these people." Those affirmations get me in the right state of mind for the job I'm about to do.

Affirmations are positive statements, usually beginning with "I," which allow you to declare what your reality will be, regardless of what it is in the moment. I've used affirmation statements for years. They help me take responsibility for the results I create, and they empower me to let go of the past and focus on what's next for me. Saying them in the mirror helps me to focus and really take them in.

Here are a few examples of positive affirmations I've used:

- *I am ready, willing, and able to manage my money wisely.*
- *I deserve to be wealthy because of the value I add to others.*
- *I am who I say I am, therefore nothing but positivity flows from my lips concerning me.*
- *The joy in my heart releases an abundance of good in my life.*

These are the kinds of affirmations I share with my community on social media, using #wealthaffirmations. What you verbalize you magnetize in your life—and in your money. Daily affirmations allow you to speak life to your desires and retrain your brain from focusing on the negative to focus on the positive and see the possibilities for your life. These short, powerful statements can help you improve your mindset about any area of your life.

Anna Lozano and Lindy Sood believe in the power of affirmations. They co-founded Love Powered Co. to create affirmation cards for their kids, and I love how their cards expand on the "I am" statement. You can do that in your affirmation practice too. You don't have to stop with a single statement. Add whatever you need to make the affirmation work for you.

A few studies have found some people not only don't respond to affirmations, but they actually feel less worthy, less deserving, or less capable after implementing a regular affirmation process. The affirmations fail to serve their purpose because they're too much of a stretch for the person saying, reading, or writing them to believe. In some cases, that seeming implausibility causes the person to spiral into negative thinking because they believe those positive affirmations couldn't possibly apply to them. They see themselves as failing at affirmations, which make them feel worse.

Sometimes, you may need to go from negative to neutral before you jump all the way to positive. If you find yourself frustrated by your affirmations or beating yourself up because you can't believe the positive things you're saying to yourself, try adding "It's possible" or "I'm working on" to your affirmation. For instance, if your brain continues to reject "I am beautiful and happy," try instead "I am a little more beautiful and a little happier every day." If you can't quite believe "I am proud of myself," try "I am working on becoming proud of myself."

Affirmations don't change your life for you. They help you shift your mindset so you can take the action that will bring what you're affirming into your life. Your affirmations are constant reminders of what's possible for you when you take right action.

REDEFINE WEALTH FOR YOURSELF

*Redefine Wealth for Yourself*
Follow the steps below to write a few affirmations of your own or
grab a set from lovepoweredco.com. Read them out loud every
day, while looking at yourself in the mirror. If you need to, take
baby steps with affirmations that stretch you a little, and then
build on those to reach the level of thought you want to achieve.

Reflect on your doubts, including the negative things you say or
think about yourself and your ability to achieve everything you
want in life, and turn them around. Focus on what you want,
rather than what you lack or are afraid of in your life. Use the
examples below to get started.

Thought: I never have enough money.
Affirmation: I enjoy a life of abundant wealth.
Thought: I can't afford it.
Affirmation: Everything I desire is available to me.
Thought: Nobody understands me or what I'm trying to do
with my life.

Affirmation: I am surrounded by people who support me in
creating my wealthy life.

# 11. PUT YOURSELF IN YOUR ASPIRATIONAL REALITY

Before you can achieve it, you have to imagine it. When I started speaking
all over the country, I quickly saw the benefits of flying first class to events
and engagements. I aspired to travel in first class all the time, but I wasn't
there yet. By 2014, I was requesting first-class travel whenever I booked
speaking gigs. If the event producer wasn't willing to accommodate my
request, I upgraded myself even if it meant simply paying the difference in
fare, hunting for deals, or sweet-talking gate agents. I wanted to physically
put myself in a reality I grew up believing was out of reach.

Eventually, I made first-class air travel a requisite part of speaking at any event. I quickly got used to other people paying for my first-class travel, but then I had to do some mindset work to travel the same way when I was just traveling for my own purposes. Now, I travel first class for business and for pleasure. I believe this is my life because I was willing to teach the universe how to see me. I consistently required it of others and of myself until what was once an aspiration became my reality.

Putting yourself in your aspirational reality isn't just a tool for travel. My college mentor Rushion McDonald explained how he consistently patronizes the same high-quality businesses. The owners and employees recognize his face, know him by name, and give him the kind of special treatment reserved for loyal customers. In this way, he was treated like a millionaire well before he became one.

Gerald and I have applied Rushion's tactic. Whenever we move into a new neighborhood, we make our rounds and assess which business might fit our needs. And then we make it a practice to patronize them regularly. We make small talk with the employees, and before long, they know our faces, and then our names, and then what we like to order or how Gerald likes his shirts done. They have no idea what we do for a living or how much money we may or may not make, but they give us the royal treatment. We aspired to have a reality in which we felt respected and valued when we traded our money for a product or service, and we have it.

### Redefine Wealth for Yourself

What do you want that seems out of reach? Brainstorm twenty ways you can start to make that aspiration a part of your reality. Be creative about how you can manifest the experience you want. Barter, use points, look for deals, expand your network, test drive that car, visit open houses in the neighborhood you want to move to next, and put yourself in the right places and around the right people.

## 12. LIVE BY THE 98/2 RULE

My husband is an award-winning executive producer, but he didn't go to film or business school. He started out carrying Steve Harvey's bags and going out for his green juice. Like me, Gerald had run his own businesses prior to the recession, but when he went to work for the Harvey organization, he started at the bottom. Eventually, he got on as a low-level, uncredited production team member, but Gerald continued to advance in his career in entertainment.

It wasn't a natural talent or a special gift for production that led to his success. It was his consistent attitude of excellence. He arrived early and stayed late. He came from a place of gratitude and truly wanting to be helpful. He remained humble and appreciative. Because of those attitudes and actions, he was given an opportunity to learn the business of television production on the job. With no education in the field, his attitude was 98% of what created his success, and his first official title in production was executive producer.

Your success is determined by more than what you do. How you do it, the attitude you bring to your work, plays a huge role. When I interviewed him on my podcast, author Kelly Cardenas shared with me his philosophy that life is 98% attitude and 2% aptitude. He learned this valuable lesson from his father, and by applying it, Kelly has reached the highest levels in the beauty industry. He has been a national educator for Paul Mitchell Systems, a successful salon owner, a motivational speaker, and more. He belongs to a small, elite group of people in his industry, and Kelly is the first to say his success came from the attitude he brought to his work.

You can make up for any shortcomings you have with the energy, enthusiasm, and positivity you bring to anything you want to achieve. You'll get what you want a lot faster when you approach life with an attitude of expectation and willingness to learn. Even when things don't go your way, the 98/2 rule reminds you that your attitude toward any setback will determine what it means for you—not the event itself. Instead of giving up or drowning in self-pity, look for the lesson and the blessing. Move on to try again or pivot to something new. But don't quit and you don't get stuck. Get your attitude right and keep going.

### Redefine Wealth for Yourself

Where do you need to show up with a better attitude? Maybe you need to focus on the way you treat your spouse or the attitude you bring to maintaining your home or your work. Choose one area and commit to bringing an attitude of excellence to it every day until it becomes a habit.

## 13. JOURNAL BEFORE YOU GO TO JAIL

After my husband's infidelity in 2016, we both joined affair recovery groups to help us deal with the aftermath. Some days, I was so angry and so hurt I envisioned new ways to inflict emotional and physical pain on him! If you've ever experienced betrayal and were immediately able to send all parties thoughts of light and love, you are a better human than me and I'm proud of you. I wasn't there though. In the beginning, I even considered quitting the women's recovery group because my raw emotions threatened to overwhelm me. But if I suppressed or ignored how I felt, those emotions would find a way out sooner or later. When they did, I might hurt somebody—and I'm not cut out for jail. I stayed with the group, and I also used my journal as a tool to work through my feelings.

I've found value in journaling for years. It's a great way to organize and process my thoughts before I share them with other people. Sometimes I use journaling prompts, and sometimes I free-write whatever comes up for me. Looking back over my journals, I can see how much growth I've undergone, how many prayers were answered, and how many things that once bothered me no longer do. I see I'm stronger than I sometimes think I am, and some of the moments I thought would end me turned out to be the beginning of the best seasons of my life.

As I watched the other women in my recovery group go through similar hurt, anger, sadness, and grief, I realized our weekly meeting was the only outlet some of them had. Like I had been, they were close to boiling over. Partly joking, but completely serious, I told them, "You'd better journal before you go to jail." Rather than act destructively, I wanted the women in my group to find the same outlet I'd found in putting those emotions on paper. That warning became our group's mantra: *journal before you go to jail.*

Think of what you've done or said out of anger or brokenness. Even if the feeling was justifiable, the decision you made in that moment was likely one you wish you could change. Every day, we experience a range of emotions. When we choose not to deal with the negative side of those feelings, we often turn to overeating, overdrinking, overspending, or other numbing behaviors to escape how we feel. Left unchecked, our negative emotions may lead to arguments and lashing out. Putting those feelings on the page and acknowledging they exist can be the first step in identifying them and dealing with them. Your journal is a space where you can express your true self without fear of being judged.

Multiple studies have found expressive writing—writing about your thoughts and emotions around a given event—can reduce stress and anxiety and make it easier for you to open up about your experience.[1] If you've tried this kind of journaling in the past and found it didn't work for you, don't give up. Instead, try something different. You might want to free-write in the mornings to get your worries and anxieties out of your head and on paper, where you can deal with them from a place of logic and start your day from a place of clarity and peace.

You might dump all your worries and concerns on the page before bed each night so you can fall asleep unburdened. After writing about your problems, you might choose to brainstorm potential solutions in your journal. Or you might prefer to purchase a journal with daily prompts specific to the issues you're dealing with in your life at the moment. The only right way to journal is the way that works for you and helps you, over time, deal with life's ups and downs so you come out better on the other side.

> ### *Redefine Wealth for Yourself*
> When you're dealing with a particularly trying emotional issue—and they will come—take the time to write out what happened and how you feel about it. Document the facts and allow yourself to release your emotions on the page so you can process them and move on to dealing with the situation from a place of clarity.

## 14. WHAT IF VS. WHAT IS

Gerald's affair partner became an online stalker who tormented me relentlessly for eighteen months. She came after me on social media, and when I blocked her, she created new profiles to troll me once again. She texted me so often from blocked numbers that I thought about changing my phone number. Checking my phone or firing up my laptop became moments of torture because I never knew when or how she'd show up. I connect with much of my community through social media, so I refused to give her the satisfaction of taking down my profiles or closing my group. I refused to change the phone number I've had since cell phones were a thing. Still, I had to do something.

One day, while I was journaling, the Holy Spirit told me I needed to dissect the truth from the lies in this madness so I could name all the noise and sift through it. I drew a line down the middle of a page in my journal, and I titled the left side "What I Fear" and the right side "What I Know" (I later renamed them "What If" and "What Is"). On the left, I listed everything that scared me about the situation. On the right, I wrote everything I knew to be true about the situation but also about myself and who the Bible said I was.

As I looked over my lists, a couple of things quickly became clear. Everything in my "Fear" column was tied to what other people would think of me if they believed what my stalker said about me, not just personally, but also the lies she made up about who I was professionally. But all the truths I'd listed in my "What I Know" column were so much more powerful and meaningful than those scary possibilities.

The truth was I had a stellar reputation as a businesswoman who always operated with integrity. I also still had a good husband. He did a dumb thing, but we were still together, still fighting for our marriage. He was doing the work, and we were doing the work together. We still had a strong and loving family. The threat that someone might find out about his behavior wasn't a real threat because it didn't matter. What mattered was how we handled it.

Every time I've done this exercise since then, my truths have trumped the scary stories I made up or accepted from other people. Fear is always based on something that might or might not happen in the future, and our brains tend to go to the worst-case scenario. But when you know who you are and whose you are, when you know the truth, you know there's nothing in your reality you can't handle. Focus on what is.

### Redefine Wealth for Yourself

When a problem threatens to overwhelm you, take a moment to do the "What If vs. What Is" exercise. Divide a sheet of paper in half and label each side. Don't be dramatic about "what if" and don't underestimate "what is." Examine the truth of your life by filling in the "what if" column with your fears and the "what is" column with the facts of the situation, including who you are and whose you are.

## 15. MEDITATE AT LEAST ONCE A WEEK

I talk a lot about meditation and how it has helped me develop a fit mindset. However, I don't usually go into detail about what that looks like for me, and many people have misunderstood the kind of meditation I practice. In fact, at speaking engagements, I've been asked to lead a guided meditation and had to explain I don't practice that kind of meditation. Like many Christians, I incorporate meditation into my prayer life by focusing on a particular scripture or passage.

However, any of a variety of forms of meditation can help you develop a fit mindset.

According to trauma-informed education specialist and author of children's books on mindfulness, Amanda Lynch, meditation is closely related to prayer. Both practices are usually still and contemplative, but while prayer is a means to make contact with God, traditional meditation is a spiritual practice that allows you to make quiet contact with your inner self in the present moment and connect with your inner thoughts. Traditional meditation may involve chanting, humming, mantras, or none of the above. There are many forms of meditation, including eating meditation, walking meditation, and loving-kindness meditation.

"As a Registered Yoga Teacher," Amanda says, "I encourage my clients to use mediation as a means of self-healing, self-compassion, and self-justice. There are so many health benefits associated with meditation. Those benefits include a reduction in stress and anxiety, an improved mood and outlook, and an increase in overall happiness." While meditation is commonly associated with Buddhist monks, Amanda explains it's an easily accessible tool anyone can implement regardless of religious beliefs.

### Redefine Wealth for Yourself
Set aside time to meditate at least once a week. Start with five minutes. If you prefer a faith-based meditation practice, see Chapter 11. If you prefer a practice that allows you to connect to the present moment, look for videos, download an app with guided mediations, or find a local meditation class. Try different methods until you find the practice that works best for you.

## CHAPTER 3

# Examine Your Mental Health

A T NINE-YEARS-OLD, MY daughter told me she thought she might have Attention Deficit Hyperactivity Disorder. Reagan was having trouble focusing in class, and without telling me, she googled her symptoms and took an online ADHD self-assessment. Because she had no stigma around mental health issues or learning differences, she was able to look for solutions and talk openly with us about the problem. Because my husband and I value mental health, we acknowledged her concerns and had her evaluated right away. She didn't actually have ADHD. She had just inherited talking too much from her mama, but the important note here is that we are committed to ensuring everyone in our household has all the necessary tools for good mental health.

To prepare for prosperity—to truly walk into the wealth God has for you—you must be mentally fit. If you're not, there's a good chance one of three things will happen: 1) you'll never attract the wealthy life you desire, 2) you'll attract prosperity, but you won't hold onto it, or 3) you'll attract some material wealth, but the rest of your life will be such a mess you won't enjoy what you have.

Being high-functioning and high-achieving doesn't necessarily mean a person is mentally healthy. Good mental health requires you to deal with traumas from the past and effectively process emotions in the present. Fortunately, you can improve your mental strength, flexibility, and endurance. You can become resilient. You can overcome trauma and manage mental illness. No matter what your past looks like, you can become mentally fit.

I'm a firm believer in therapy for everyone, starting at an early age. That includes periodic check-ups with a professional who can evaluate your mental wellbeing. In some cases, improving and maintaining your mental health requires taking on new habits and letting go of old ones with the help of a life coach or counseling with a therapist. In other cases, you may need medication to deal with a mental illness, like anxiety or depression.

At lunch with a friend, I had this chapter on my mind and I brought up the subject of mental illness. My friend casually told me she'd been diagnosed with depression, anxiety, and panic disorder. She'd dealt with depression since her adolescence, and the anxiety and panic attacks had been triggered during a difficult divorce. "I was on meds for a while, and I saw a psychologist for years," she explained, "but for the most part, I manage it with lifestyle now." She went back to her salad, and our conversation moved on. It wasn't a big deal to her because she'd done what was necessary to manage her mental illness successfully.

The term "mental illness" covers a wide range of mental health conditions. It includes depression and anxiety, eating disorders (including anorexia, bulimia, and binge eating), addictive behaviors (including substance abuse), and personality and trauma-related disorders. Experts estimate almost half the people in the United States will experience some sort of mental illness in their lifetime, the effects of which can range from mild to severe.[2] We need to acknowledge and deal with mental illness, and at the same time, focus on mental wellness.

As a society, we must invest in our mental health the same way we invest in our physical health. We have to make it acceptable for adults and children to experience and process their emotions, rather than always putting on a brave face and pretending everything's cool. Once upon a time, it was considered strange to join a gym or go out for a jog. These days, working out is perfectly acceptable. In fact, in some places, you're considered odd if you don't have a regular workout routine. Treat your mental wellness as just as important as your physical fitness and health because, without it, you can never truly be wealthy.

## 16. GIVE YOURSELF PERMISSION TO FEEL

Almost every day, when Reagan gets in the car, she wants to talk about what happened at school or what's going on in her life. But sometimes, at the end of a long day, she's not in the mood for conversation. "I just don't feel like talking right now," she'll tell me. Because I've been a self-development junkie for most of my life, and because I know what it's like to be forced to suppress my feelings, I allow her the space to feel whatever's going on inside her.

As a child, it wouldn't have been acceptable for me to tell an adult I didn't feel like talking or to sit in my sadness, anger, or worry. Without any consideration for what I was experiencing, I would have been forced to talk. However, I've given my daughter the gift of being able to feel and express her emotions authentically. She doesn't have to hide her feelings or pretend to be happy for the adults in her life. Usually, Reagan will come to me later and explain what was going on with her. She needs time to feel her feelings and process them before she shares them with me.

Suppressing your emotions is like pushing a beach ball under the water. The ball keeps popping back up no matter how hard or how deep you force it down, and your emotions behave the same way. You can keep pushing them down, but eventually, anger, sadness, grief, and other feelings rise up and find a way to express themselves. You walk around irritable, snapping at people all day long, or you temporarily numb yourself with overeating, overdrinking, overspending, losing yourself on social media, or other self-harming or unproductive behaviors. The stress of denying your feelings can also show up in the body as disease. The symptoms may be high blood pressure, high cholesterol, obesity, or something else, but sooner or later, the suffering shows itself in our behaviors, in our relationships, and in our bodies.

It's our nature to express our emotions, but many of us have been taught not to show how we really feel. We've become so steeped in the power of positive thinking we may feel shame when we have a negative emotion and avoid actually feeling it. Believers often get the message that we should just pray about it, and if we're praying about it, we shouldn't be sad about it. Society, including well-meaning parents who may have rushed in to solve our problems before we became too upset, has convinced us we shouldn't ever feel bad.

Yes, you should be grateful. You should think positively, and you should pray if you're a person of faith, but none of that negates the fact that you're a human being who experiences the full spectrum of human emotions. Even if you don't express them or process them, they're inside you, and they will find a way to express themselves. You can't escape your feelings, but you can experience them and still go about creating wealth unencumbered by suppressed suffering.

When I interviewed life coach and spiritual psychologist Christine Hassler on *Redefining Wealth*, she explained that when you try to avoid or suppress your feelings, they come out in "leaky ways." Christine explains, "When you suppress the negative feelings, you have less access to joy, creativity, and passion." It's hard to live a wealthy life without those things. But for many of us, connecting with what we're feeling is easier said than done because we've spent a lifetime being trained not to do it.

Our culture has randomly defined which emotions men and women are allowed to feel. It's perfectly acceptable for men to demonstrate anger within the limits of the law, but they're often judged if they exhibit sadness. Women, on the other hand, are often given the message early in life that anger isn't ladylike or acceptable for them to express. Many Black women are hyper aware of the stereotype of the angry Black woman and are hesitant to express anger, lest they be labeled as such. Both men and women experience the full range of emotions, but all too often don't know how to express or process them.

Christine suggests an exercise of giving your emotions names so you can show those parts of yourself more compassion. I've started practicing this in my life. When Anxious Angela shows up, I remind myself to have compassion for her. "Compassion has zero judgment and zero analysis," Christine says. When I greet Anxious Angela with compassion, there's no room for me to judge or criticize myself for having that feeling.

If you're accustomed to denying, ignoring, or suppressing your emotions, give yourself permission to feel, first by learning to acknowledge and identify your emotions. Then, allow yourself to feel them without criticism or judgment. If you're sad, be sad. Cry when you need to cry. Go take a boxing class if you need a place to release your anger. Find ways to express those emotions so you can process them and move on. Don't judge them. Don't analyze them. Just feel.

### Redefine Wealth for Yourself

Take a few minutes to journal each day. Write about whatever events or circumstances are on your mind and describe how they make you feel. If you find it difficult to express your feelings, seek the assistance of a therapist who can give you tools to process your emotions.

## 17. STOP SUFFERING IN SILENCE

Sonya (not her real name) told our mastermind group, "I don't actually sleep at night," as if this were a normal way to function. At first, I thought she meant she was #teamnosleep. I was under the impression that she was hustling and grinding, pushing herself to work at all hours in an effort to create her version of success. However, five months later on our mastermind retreat, I found out that wasn't Sonya's story.

During a session in which some of the women spoke of trauma they'd experienced, Sonya blurted out, "They would touch me if I went to sleep!" She hadn't enjoyed a good night's sleep in twenty years because, as a child, falling asleep had made her vulnerable to male relatives who molested her. Instead, she trained herself to stay awake. In school, her grades fell because she showed up every day sleep deprived. As an adult, she found herself hopping from job to job, never able to give her best because she was perpetually exhausted.

Sonya hadn't told her husband, her adult children, or anyone else what had been done to her. She'd suffered, all those years, in silence. However, the day after she shared it with the group, she told us that, for the first time she could remember, she'd slept six straight hours. Simply by sharing her story and getting support and encouragement, she was finally able to get some much-needed rest. Since then, I've watched her blossom in her business and personal life, all because she finally found a safe space to share the burden she'd carried alone for two decades.

Most of the shame we carry is rooted in the fear that people will judge us and think less of us if they know our truth. I've carried my own suffering in silence. For years, I rarely told anyone that, exactly one year before I had Reagan, I gave birth to a baby boy who weighed one pound and lived for less than five hours. Clutching my index finger in his tiny hand, he took his last breath while I held him in my arms. For so long, I didn't talk about the son we lost before we had Reagan. Because I had grief counseling, I knew I shouldn't blame myself, but thoughts of what I could've done differently still bubbled up in my mind on occasion. I judged myself, and I imagined other people would judge me too. It took years for me to start acknowledging I had a child before Reagan.

Because I didn't talk about my loss outside of counseling, I felt alone with it, as if other people couldn't understand my suffering. I wondered what was wrong with me that my baby would be taken from me. But when I started to share my story, I discovered so many women around me had experienced similar losses. Family members told me about babies they'd lost. Friends shared their stories of miscarriages.

When I stopped suffering in silence, I realized I wasn't alone in my experience. In fact, I discovered what I'd gone through wasn't unusual at all. If we knew how many babies are conceived that never make it here, those of us with healthy children would understand how truly fortunate we are. Every time a baby makes it here healthy and whole, it's a miracle.

I've spoken of my pain publicly, in videos, from the stage, on the podcast, and now, in this book. I live much of my life on a public platform, and as I teach people how to live a truly wealthy life, I want them to see and be inspired by what I've gone through. But you don't have to tell everyone your story to stop suffering in silence. There's no need to post it on social media or call a family meeting unless that's right for you. You might only tell the people closest to you or a therapist, but you must give voice to your suffering so you can start to deal with it. Left unspoken, suffering can lead to depression, anxiety, and even suicide. It's all so unnecessary when, in many instances, simply saying it out loud could provide you the relief you seek.

### Redefine Wealth for Yourself

Take an honest look at yourself. Are you suffering in silence? Are you carrying around pain you can't speak about or overcome? If your answer is yes, make a decision to get professional help to address the issue. If your immediate answer is no because you don't think you've experienced anything "that bad," dig a little deeper and stop comparing your trauma to other people's pain. Do you have any of the results of silent suffering, like overeating, overdrinking, or overspending, in your life? If so, find a therapist who can help you get to the root of the problem.

## 18. DON'T BE AFRAID TO SIT ON THE COUCH

One day, when I was a little girl, I walked into our home after school and found my grandmother and another adult engaged in conversation. Like the well-raised girl I was, I said "Good afternoon," but before I knew what was happening, I felt a sharp slap across my face. My grandmother was saying something, clearly chastising me, but I couldn't hear her. I was too shocked by the slap that had come out of nowhere, knocking my head to one side and bringing tears, hot and plentiful, to my eyes.

I experienced the same humiliating punishment many times. I would never be so foolish as to come into the house and not speak to any adult present. She demanded all her grandchildren mind a strict set of manners, and I was an obedient child. But sometimes, I didn't speak loudly enough, and if she didn't hear me clearly, then my greeting didn't count. Without trying to, I had disrespected her, which earned me a slap across the face every single time.

In my early adulthood, my friends would talk about the spankings they'd gotten as children, and I considered myself lucky I'd never been spanked. It didn't occur to me to relate getting slapped in the face to spanking and certainly not to physical abuse. In many ways, the slaps were worse than a spanking, which when we were growing up, could be classified as discipline. A slap in the face was much more personal and painful. It was more about satisfying the person doing the slapping than about teaching the one on the receiving end a lesson. It was dehumanizing, and to inflame the insult, it often happened in front of other people.

Only in therapy did I start to dig up and understand the abuses I'd endured as a child. I'd normalized the kind of mistreatment I'd never allow anyone to inflict on my own child. I'd heard so many stories of children who went through so much worse that I minimized my own suffering. I had to reevaluate some of my childhood experiences. Through the help of a counselor, I realized the complete lack of privacy, which included men using the bathroom while I sat in the bathtub next to the toilet, an early exposure to pornography, and the way my grandmother tore me down with her words all constituted forms of abuse.

I, like so many innocent Children in drug-infested neighborhoods, experienced traumatic events on a regular basis. I witnessed a dead body lying still on the sidewalk after a drive-by shooting. I watched people in my neighborhood actively using drugs, and I saw my brother shot and bleeding. While those events didn't paralyze me or prevent me from moving forward and achieving great things in my life, they each affected me in some way. By addressing them in therapy, I was able to understand how those events altered the way I saw myself and the world.

Recently, I turned down a woman who wanted to join my mastermind group because I believed she needed therapy before she could be effective in my program. I said to her several times on our discovery call, "I don't think you need a business coach. I think you need a life coach or therapist." Business coaching is great, but your business coach cannot be your therapist. Most of us aren't licensed or equipped to help you deal with trauma or the other issues a licensed psychologist, psychiatrist, or therapist can help you manage and overcome.

So many people shy away from therapy, but your success may be on the other side of sitting on someone's couch. There's still significant stigma surrounding therapy, particularly in communities of color, which is why so many people walk around like ticking time bombs, waiting to explode. Maybe you're afraid to get the therapy you're in need of. Or maybe you believe achieving your goals means you've gotten over your trauma. However, everyone can benefit from the assistance of a good therapist to deal with past trauma, develop stronger coping skills, or manage the challenges we face in life right at this moment. Regular check-ups with a mental health professional can elevate your mental wellbeing.

If you don't have a therapist near you or you need appointments outside of normal business hours, check out some of the apps that can connect you to a therapist. If you don't have money in your budget for therapy, look for therapists who charge on a sliding scale or find low-cost or no-cost support groups. Don't give up if the first therapist you contact isn't right for you. I once went to a therapist who made a comment that made me uncomfortable in our first session. I didn't go back to him, but I didn't give up on therapy either. I kept looking for someone I felt comfortable talking with, and I eventually found the right person. Therapy requires you to be vulnerable to another human being, and you have to feel safe in the relationship.

> ### Redefine Wealth for Yourself
> Find a therapist. Do your research, ask for referrals, and be willing to try more than one professional. If you're dealing with a particular issue, find a specialist in that area. Make an appointment and sit on the couch.

## 19. EMBRACE GRIEF WITH GRACE

Simone (not her real name), a member of my Mastery + Momentum mastermind group, had a quiet, capable demeanor. Not only did she carry herself as a strong Black woman, she always showed up looking so put together. While I might be on a video conference with no makeup and wearing a baseball cap, Simone's face was always beat. Looking at her, I thought she was doing well, that she had it all together.

During our mastermind retreat, we discussed the PEOPLE pillar and Simone finally revealed the pain behind her perfectly made-up face. She had lost her mother and her sister, one right after the other, and losing her sister nearly took her out. She felt guilty having female friends because her sister had been her best friend. Taking trips with women and laughing and talking for hours with girlfriends made Simone feel guilty for being alive when her mother and sister were gone and like she was betraying her sister's friendship.

Simone joined our group, which was billed as creating a sisterhood, to try to move past her resistance to having close relationships with women. She was one of several women to come to the mastermind while dealing with the grief of losing a woman-to-woman relationship with a mother, a sister, or a friend. Difficulty dealing with that grief had shut them down and caused them to build a wall. They avoided friendships with women because they were afraid to suffer the same kind of loss again.

Grief is a deep sense of sorrow, a normal reaction to loss or change of some kind. We often think of grief in terms of losing a loved one, but it can be a natural response to many other situations, including the death of a pet, the loss of a job, divorce, bankruptcy, moving away from a place you know and love, or even the experience of self-quarantine we all shared during the COVID-19 pandemic of 2020.

According to the Grief Recovery Institute, "Grief is the conflicting feelings caused by the end of or change in a familiar pattern of behavior."[3] Imagine the woman who loses her father after caring for him through his prolonged illness. She may be devastated by the loss, but she may also feel relieved her father is no longer suffering. The woman who receives a promotion may be excited about the opportunity and still grieve the fact that she'll no longer be in the same department with co-workers she loves. Those conflicting emotions are all a part of grieving.

Learning to process grief is an essential life skill because loss is a universal constant. Mourning a loss is normal, but when you're mourning what could have been or what once was, it may be hard to find the focus and energy to create a wealthy life. Sometimes, grief can become overwhelming. The person grieving becomes numb to life, isolates herself, or drops out of social activities. More often, however, we put on a pretty face, show up the way we're expected to, and stay busy, so we look like we're healed. As with Simone, the effects of prolonged grieving aren't always visible to the outside world. Embracing grief with grace will help you process it in the healthiest possible way and enter a stage of grief recovery.

Psychiatrist Elisabeth Kubler-Ross identified the five stages of grief as: denial, anger, bargaining, depression, and acceptance. However, I spoke with licensed clinical social work and grief recovery specialist Herdyne Mercier who explained that, while some people may go through those stages, current research has found most people don't experience grief in that way. Some people, for example, never reach a state of acceptance. You may have experienced grief without ever feeling angry, falling into depression, or trying to bargain with God. Any of the five stages is possible, but not necessarily a part of everyone's experience.

Our society as a whole doesn't deal well with grief. Many people get the message early in life that we're not supposed to show emotion. Men are taught to be strong and that real men don't cry. Black women are taught, directly or indirectly, to hold themselves to the standard of the "strong Black woman." Employers offer three-day bereavement leave, implying you should be over it by the time that period ends. When someone you know is grieving, it's often hard to know what to do or say to help, and when you're grieving, the people who care about you may not know how to help you either. You have to be willing to find and ask for the support you need.

With grief, there's not necessarily an end to the journey, but you can enter a state of grief recovery. Once you've processed that grief you may still find yourself triggered and once again having an emotional reaction to that loss months or even years later. The anniversary of a death or events that take you back to a loss may reignite those feelings of grief. That's perfectly normal.

Embracing grief with grace requires you to first acknowledge that you've suffered a loss and name how you feel about it. Say what you feel. Don't keep it to yourself. Find someone who's willing to listen. Understand it may take weeks, months, or years for you to process your grief. If you don't have anyone in your circle to confide in, or your need deeper help, seek assistance from a grief specialist.

> ### Redefine Wealth for Yourself
> When you're grieving, don't rush the process. Allow yourself to feel whatever emotions come up. Ask someone you trust to hear you without judgment—your sister circle, partner, a compassionate relative—to listen while you share what you're feeling. If you need help processing your grief, seek help from a grief recovery specialist.

## 20. ACCEPT THE LUXURY OF HEALING

As a single mom, my mother worked hard to take care of our family, but that meant there were many times she couldn't be present when I wanted her to be. Because of the way I grew up, I created a story about the kind of mother I would be when it was my turn. I didn't realize it at the time, but I set a completely unrealistic standard for myself and discounted my husband's role in raising our daughter. In the process, I was unintentionally recreating my childhood—single mother doing it all, father uninvolved and not present—for my daughter.

Early in Reagan's life, I thought I had to do everything. I had to attend every performance, school event, and activity, even if it meant missing something important to me. I had to drop her off at school, pick her up from school, and do homework with her. I had to take her to every doctor's appointment. To be a good mom, I thought, I had to do it all. It would have been nearly impossible for a stay-at-home mom to meet my standard, and I was working full-time, building a business, and helping my family recover from the recession at that time.

Gerald, on the other hand, never felt like he had to be present for every moment of our child's life. While I made everything important, even when it wasn't, he showed up for the things that mattered to him and felt no guilt for missing the rest. It didn't take long for me to start to resent his laid-back parenting approach. I was overwhelmed and wearing myself out, and he wasn't. I thought my husband should look at me and know I needed help. I didn't think I should have to say, "Can you please pick up Reagan from school today?" when I had something else to do. I wanted him to magically know what I needed. And that was never going to happen.

In truth, I had no idea how a family with two engaged parents functioned. I was raised by single mothers, and in fact, I was the first woman on my mother's side of the family to get married. My aunts and female cousins, my mother, and my grandmother, they all raised their families and ran their households without husbands. I'd broken that cycle, but not completely. I wasn't a single mother, but I was living as if I was. My mother and grandmother did it all because they had to do it all. If they didn't do a thing, then it wasn't going to get done. I had taken on the same burden even though I had a husband willing and able to help me.

Our family dynamic of two married parents raising a child together was new to me, and it showed. If Gerald offered to do something for me, I had an attitude about how or when he offered. If he didn't read my mind and know I needed help, I told myself he was selfish and unreliable. One day, I felt overwhelmed and finally blew up at him. Totally confused, Gerald asked me, "Babe, why didn't you just tell me you needed help?" It finally dawned on me that I didn't have to live the way my mother and grandmother lived. I had options they didn't have.

When I talked with licensed psychologist, ordained minister, and sacred artist Dr. Thema Bryant-Davis on my podcast, she pointed out that most of our mothers and grandmothers didn't have access to the healing tools available to us. They didn't have the luxury of shifting from surviving to thriving. For my family of immigrant women, who still supported their extended family back home, tools like therapy, meditation, and journaling would've seemed like a waste of time. Those things weren't a part of their world. My life, as it is now, allows me those luxuries. I have the option to heal.

Of course, learning to ask my husband for help made my life easier. These days, he cleans more than I do, and he does all our home cooking. He volunteers to go to the grocery store, and we take turns driving Reagan to wherever she needs to be. We're a team. Everything that needs to get done gets done, and I don't have the overwhelm or the attitude I had when I was trying to do it all by myself.

Accepting the luxury of healing also allowed Reagan and her father to form a special bond that would've been hard to create if she'd spent all her time with me. They have private, just-between-us conversations to which I'm not privy. They have their own routine, like stopping at Starbucks when Gerald drives her to school. They have the kind of closeness I want my daughter to have with her father, and while we're a family, their relationship is independent of me.

Maybe you don't have a problem asking for help, but we all have areas where we need healing. Healing is an ongoing process, but the more you do it, the better you'll get at it, and the closer you'll be to living your wealthy life. Healing is a luxury you deserve.

### *Redefine Wealth for Yourself*

Where in your life are you not allowing yourself to heal or get help? What story are you holding onto that's no longer yours—or was never yours in the first place? Decide to give yourself the luxury of healing. Commit to getting better and seek professional help if you need it.

# PART II. PEOPLE

## Create Relationships That Matter

WHEN *THE OPRAH Winfrey Show* was on the air, it seemed like every ambitious person dreamed of landing a spot on the couch. If they could just get on Oprah, their book would be a bestseller. If she chose their product for her "Favorite Things" list, sales would finally skyrocket. If Oprah blessed their business, she'd make them an overnight success. These were the stories people told themselves as they fantasized, plotted, and planned for their big break with the queen of daytime talk.

While it's never a good idea to depend on one long-shot strategy for your success, there was nothing inherently wrong with wanting to leverage "the Oprah effect" to launch you to success. However, some people were so laser-focused on making that one relationship happen that they overlooked, dismissed, and diminished the relationships in their own circles. In doing so, they missed out on opportunities that could've helped them achieve what they wanted.

In the pursuit of achievement, it's easy to forget how important relationships—personal and professional—can be in creating your wealthy life. Even if you land a game-changing opportunity, your relationships will determine whether or not you can make the most of it. As a business owner, your relationships with vendors, team members, and customers need to be solid if you want to grow. If your family life isn't in order, any opportunity or blessing you get can become a curse when success burdens already strained relationships.

One of the keys to my ability to build wealth is my unwavering stance that relationships mean something to me. The people I've met along the way helped to shape my view of the world and taught me valuable lessons. I've had allies and enemies, and learning to navigate that terrain to take care of relationships that matter is why I'm here. Without the people I'm in community with, I would have nothing. Without my family and friends, what I have would mean nothing.

The PEOPLE pillar follows the FIT pillar because relationships are fundamental to true wealth. Without strong professional ties, earning more is much more difficult than it needs to be. When your family relationships fall apart, no amount of money can fix them. Fortunately, you have the power to create and sustain relationships that matter. With the principles in this section, you can repair damaged relationships, start new ones, and build unbreakable bonds with the people who mean the most in your life.

## CHAPTER 4

# Protect Personal Relationships First

I'D JUST RETURNED home after several days away on a book tour. Three times in one day, my daughter, who was six at the time, called me by the nanny's name. Each time, Reagan quickly corrected herself, but each time, the mistake stung. I'd been on the road, traveling all over the country, but I didn't think I'd been gone long enough for my child to forget who I was. Of course, Reagan still knew her mother, but that day, it felt like I had traded my role in my child's life for my career.

I had no doubt my daughter loved me and felt loved by me, but I had to ask myself if I was putting my time and attention in the right place. Because I worked most of the time from my home office, I saw myself as present and available for her. In reality, when I was in my home office, I was focused on work, not on Reagan. I asked myself if I was chasing money and opportunity at the cost of my relationship with my child.

As my new business took off, I developed a lot of mom guilt. I wasn't sure I was making the right choices. I wondered if it was selfish to leave my family for days at a time. I wondered if I was really called to this work in the first place. After all, God had blessed me with a daughter and a husband, and I was out there trying to be America's Money Maven on top of all that.

I couldn't truly embrace my calling to be Reagan's mom, Gerald's wife, and America's Money Maven all at the same time until I started to clean up and heal my personal relationships. I had to put them in their proper place. I didn't want to be a public success and a private failure, so I got intentional about improving my home life, family connections, and friendships. Learning to protect my personal relationships first freed me to excel in my business. Once I made it clear they were my priority, my family supported me even more, and because I implement the principles in this chapter, I no longer feel guilty about the time I'm away from them. Today, my family gives me the strength to go out and give one hundred percent to everything I do.

In *The Joy of Missing Out*, Tanya Dalton says, "We have to begin finding the joy of missing out on that extra noise in our lives and instead find happiness in a life centered on what's truly important to us."[4] When it comes down to it, personal relationships are, or should be, truly important to us. They cannot be put on hold while we chase money or success. To truly have wealth, or wellbeing, you must protect personal relationships first.

## 21. HONOR YOUR PERSONAL COMMITMENTS

In 2019, I traveled to Mexico with a group of amazing women to celebrate the fortieth birthday of our friend Marshawn Evans Daniels. We had a detailed itinerary with start times for each activity, and one evening, one of the guests reminded us all we needed to be ready at 7:55 for the excursion the next morning. At that moment, another guest, LaShawne Holland, turned to me and said, "But for you, that's 7:00 a.m."

Admittedly, I'd been a few minutes late to every event, but I explained to LaShawne that, while I sometimes run late for personal matters, I'm always on time for professional commitments. "Of course, you are," she said. "You wouldn't be where you are if you weren't on time professionally."

Our brief exchange stuck with me. LaShawne was right. I was where I was in my professional life because of how I showed up, and that included being punctual. But for every personal event, I showed up a few minutes late, and it negatively impacted my personal relationships. Five minutes here, fifteen minutes there—I was consistently last to arrive. Friends and family didn't ask me to bring anything important to an event because they knew I'd be late. Essentially they couldn't depend on me.

Pastor Andy Stanley pointed out in a sermon how most of us save our best behavior for professional relationships. We send our best representative to conduct business, but we get too relaxed with family and friends. We treat personal commitments as if they're less important. You can't pretend, Pastor Stanley noted, that you don't know how to behave because if you were having dinner with the person you'd most like to sit down with, you'd be on your best behavior. If I had dinner plans with Michelle Obama, I'd arrive no less than an hour early. Period.

It's easy to hold yourself to a high standard at work or in your business because your money and your professional reputation are at stake. You might receive a bad review, lose a client, or be overlooked for the next opportunity if you don't bring your best self to your work. The consequences of being less concerned and diligent in your personal life aren't always so obvious. Instead, when you fail to honor your personal commitments, your relationships and the expectations people have of you erode over time.

Showing up late isn't the only way people fail to honor their personal commitments. Maybe you pay all your bills on time, but you still haven't repaid your friend for the Uber ride she covered months ago. Maybe you keep promising to go to church with your grandmother, but every week, you find a reason to sleep in instead. Maybe you swear you're going to volunteer in your niece's classroom, but it keeps slipping your mind. If you're like most high-achievers, you'd never drop the ball like that at work or in your business. Choose to honor your personal commitments in the same way. Your relationships will grow stronger, and you'll have the satisfaction of knowing the people closest to you see you as dependable and consistent.

> **Redefine Wealth for Yourself**
> List all the commitments you've made in your personal life.
> Decide whether you'll recommit to, renegotiate, or release
> each one. Talk to the people involved with the commitments
> you need to release or renegotiate. If you recommit to a task,
> schedule a time and set reminders to make sure you get it done
> as promised. Finally, block the time to honor your ongoing
> personal commitments.

## 22. LISTEN LIKE YOU CARE

Reagan was trying to tell me a story, but while I wanted to look like I was, I wasn't really listening. At one point, she told me what had happened and I laughed and nodded in agreement, but she wasn't fooled. "That wasn't a good thing I just told you," she said. "You're not listening." If you have children or have spent time with children, you know they sometimes talk in circles and tell really long stories, and it's easy for us as adults to discount how significant the story is to them because they're not telling it fast enough for us. All too often, we try to make them think we're listening when we're really doing something we think is more important in the moment. Sadly, they always know when we're checked out on the conversation.

Kids aren't the only ones feeling unheard. In 2018, the Capital One Listen In Survey found 18% of Americans can't remember the last time they felt likes someone really focused on listening to them. More than half the respondents (51%) said their friends, family, and colleagues fail to actively listen to them. Being heard makes us feel significant, accepted, and important. It's a basic psychological need, and when it's not met by the people closest to us, those relationships suffer.

Of course, there are times when you can't give your loved one your undivided attention, and it's perfectly okay to tell them so. The reason Reagan feels so supported and in turn supports me at this stage in her life is because I've learned to actively listen to her and show her I care about what she's saying. When I can't listen right away, I explain I have something else to do and ask her to wait until I can give her my full attention. I really want to hear her whole story, not just pretend to listen. Even at a young age, she understood and respected my explanation.

To protect your personal relationships, you have to make sure the people in your life feel heard by you. When friends or family members talk to you, set aside any distractions. Make eye contact as much as possible. Listen to the facts and pay attention to how they feel about those facts. Let them share as much as they want before you add your comments, questions, or opinions. Make them feel like there's no place else you'd rather be and nothing you'd rather be doing.

### Redefine Wealth for Yourself

Make it a habit to put down your phone and close your laptop when you want to have a personal conversation. If it's not a good time to listen, ask your loved one to talk with you later, at an agreed upon time.

## 23. ENFORCE STRONG BOUNDARIES

April Pace, one of the members of Mastery + Momentum, doesn't mess around with her boundaries. Her friends and family know if they have an event on a Sunday, for example, April won't be there. Sundays are sacred to her, and she has communicated this to the people closest to her. She uses the day to plan and prepare for the week ahead, including meal prepping, selecting the week's outfits, and getting organized to take on work tasks. She's firm with this boundary because she realizes that relaxing it one time would open the floodgates for others to disrespect the time she's carved out for herself. She's also pregnant with our first M+M baby as I write this, and these boundaries will serve her well as a new mother.

To protect personal relationships and honor your personal commitments, put boundaries in place. In her book, *Boss Bride*, international speaker, coach, and former *Essence* senior editor, Charreah Jackson says, "People don't treat you how you treat them. People treat you how you treat yourself. When you love on yourself and enforce your boundaries, you teach others to do the same." Boundaries are an act of self-love and self-care, and when you choose to honor them, it makes the people and things you choose to allow in your life that much sweeter. You have a right to require people to treat you how you want to be treated.

Boundaries allow you to spell out what's acceptable to you. People can then choose to honor your limits or accept the consequences. Your boundaries define how you're willing to spend your most precious resources, including your money, time, and energy, what you will and will not accept in your life, and how you'll respond if someone fails to respect those boundaries.

You can't necessarily stop a friend from raising her voice at you, for example, but you can set the boundary: "When you raise your voice at me, I will end our phone call or leave your presence." You get to decide if you want to actually say that to your friend or not. You can choose to share it with her or keep the new boundary to yourself and quietly enforce it. She may never stop yelling at you, but you'll no longer have to tolerate the undesirable behavior in your life when you set and stick to your boundary.

Many of my clients feel guilty when they start to set boundaries. They see boundaries as a punishment for people or a way of putting themselves above others. However, that isn't the case. Personal boundaries are parameters you set to define acceptable ways for people to treat you and how you'll choose to respond when their behavior falls outside of those parameters. Healthy personal boundaries aren't designed to sow division or cut people out of your life. Instead, they define who is worthy of staying *in* your life.

*Redefine Wealth for Yourself*
When you don't have a lot of practice doing it, setting boundaries can be daunting. Follow this template to make those difficult conversations easier to have:

*I apologize for leading you to believe for the last few* (days weeks, months, years) *that* (behavior) *was acceptable to me. The truth is when you do* (behavior), *I feel* (emotion), *and feeling that way isn't acceptable to me anymore. Thank you for understanding.*

## 24. SAY "NO" WITH ENTHUSIASM

As I was checking out of the grocery store one day, the cashier asked me to make a donation to March of Dimes. The organization is close to my heart because of my experiences having premature babies. However, I declined to donate that day. "I hope you never have a child with this kind of problem," the cashier said.

This woman had no idea I'd already given birth to two premature children, one of whom didn't make it home from the hospital. She didn't know I was already a regular contributor to March of Dimes and had already given $1000 to the organization that year. I could have explained all that to her, but my no doesn't require explanation. I'm not moved by her opinion of me. I give what I want, when I want, and I won't be pressured into impulse giving.

Observe any toddler and you'll quickly see how simple it is to say no with enthusiasm and without concern for what people will think of you. My good friend Karli Harvey Raymond's preschool-aged son, BJ, regularly says no to requests and goes about his day without giving it another thought. He doesn't waste time trying to clean it up or explain. His no stands on its own. He says no to what you want him to do so he can do what he wants instead.

Sometimes you have to say no to other people so you can say yes to yourself. You don't have to be coldhearted. When its warranted, you can even explain your no. But to stay focused on what you're doing, you have to stop getting sucked into everyone else's vision or their opinions of your vision. Stop worrying people will think you're selfish or mean if you turn down a request. Let your no come from a place of saying yes to investing your time and money in your priorities.

My granny used to say, "Let your yes be your yes and your no be your no." To get to that place, start with baby steps and practice saying no with the enthusiasm of a two-year-old. If you're accustomed to saying yes before you think through the costs, practice first with small things. Build up to saying no with enthusiasm to requests you don't want to fulfill or which distract you from your priorities.

### Redefine Wealth for Yourself

Follow my 5-step process to say no and still leave the person making the request with his or her dignity:

1. Detach yourself from the outcome and avoid making up stories about how you think people will react.
2. Acknowledge the request and the courage it may have taken to make it.
3. Offer a clear decline and leave no ambiguity about your response.
4. Avoid lengthy explanations and let your no stand on its own.
5. Accept whatever response you receive to your no.

## 25. DON'T BE ABOVE BACKING OUT

As a classic overachiever, my natural tendency is to complicate things. I have a lot of ideas, and in the past, I'd often layer one thing on top of another, not realizing I was overwhelming myself, my team, and my audience. In 2018, I realized anything that wasn't my purpose work had to come off my calendar. At our team retreat, I realized how important it was to me to create community at that stage of my life. In talking to the Seek Wisdom Find Wealth team, which included my husband, I realized they were all on board to help me bring my vision to life. However, I also got clarity around the fact that I could not do everything I wanted to do and create the community I dreamed of having. Some of the events and activities I'd already committed to would have to come off my agenda. I was going to have to back out of them to clear the way for what really mattered to me.

If your days are already filled with work and family commitments, you might have to back out of the commitment you made to serve on the board of a nonprofit or bake cookies for the PTA. Yes, somebody may need to do those things, but that somebody doesn't have to be you. You could be pouring into your family and your most important relationships during those hours. If those commitments aren't in alignment with your purpose and you're doing them out of a sense of obligation or guilt, you're probably better off backing out and allowing someone else to step in and fill in the gap with joy.

Sometimes, we say yes even when a part of us knows we should say no. We agree because we don't want conflict, or because we have a fear of abandonment, or because we want to be liked. Those reactions are human nature, but sometimes, you have to circle back and say, "I said I would, but I thought about it, and I'm not going to be able to do it." You have to detach yourself from the outcome. There's a chance that person will think less of you or not like you anymore, but if you back out gracefully, and they have a negative response, that's not your business. Be okay with the result.

When you don't have enough time to do all the things that are important to you, back out of things that don't matter as much so you can focus on rebuilding or maintaining your personal relationships. Many women spend more time volunteering with the church, their children's school and sports teams, and their favorite nonprofits than they spend connecting with their partner or their kids. Because we're taught it's good to serve, they dedicate more time to volunteer work than they do to building their dream business. Don't let people make you feel guilty about not wanting to be a career volunteer. There will be different seasons in your life when you have more or less time to give, and you're not wrong for wanting to focus on what's most important to you at any given moment.

### Redefine Wealth for Yourself

Take a look at your calendar and assess the commitments you have coming up. Choose to back out of those that aren't aligned with your purpose and take time and energy from the personal relationships you want to prioritize.

## CHAPTER 5

# Surround Yourself with
# the Right People

UTHOR, SPEAKER, AND coach Suzette Vearnon had been a
Lone Ranger, figuring out how to create the life and business
she wanted on her own for years. One day, she was onstage at
a live event when she heard God tell her, "Bigger stages." On her first
Purpose 2 Platform call, she told us about her experience and how she
felt it was time to create her own event. Suzette had only been in the
program for a week, and my initial response to her was: "Let's get through
the modules first."

Suzette was committed to doing the work, but she was also determined to be obedient to the call she felt on her life. Here's the thing: if
I'd been coaching her one-on-one, I would've tried to protect her from
losing money on an event I didn't think she was ready for by coaching
her out of the idea. But she didn't just have me. She had a community.
On the group call, other women popped up in the chat box to find out
where Suzette lived and how they could support her. Later, she went
into the online group and listed everything she needed for her event.
Within forty-eight hours, other members had come together and met
every need she had.

Suzette applied everything she learned in Purpose 2 Platform, and not two months later, in time for her sixtieth birthday, she held her first live event. Fellow members of the program reviewed her plan and her marketing materials and gave her feedback along the way. On the day of the event, four group members drove from other states to support her. They had committed to being there, and they showed up for her.

So many people come to me looking for one-on-one coaching. They think their situation is special and unique. They think nobody has ever been where they are and the only way they'll achieve what they want is to have the undivided attention of a coach. I used to think the same way. I sought individual coaching and prided myself on coaching clients one on one. But as I grew as a coach and experienced the power of community, I discovered the unexpected benefits of receiving coaching in a group and having a network of people to support you on your journey.

I created Purpose 2 Platform to give spirit-led, purpose-driven entrepreneurs the knowledge they need to monetize their God-given gifts while they impact the world in positive ways. However, I also wanted to create a community where they could connect with like-minded heart-led women, grow together, and support each other in their efforts. I'm their coach, so it can be hard for them to imagine doing everything I do. However, as they watch their peers absorbing information and applying it, they see what's possible for them in a real way. In addition, I'm only one person, but in their community, they have a wealth of resources, including people to hold them accountable and encourage them.

The right people, the ones you need to surround yourself with, may be at the conference you've been researching for years but never invested in attending. The peers who will hold you accountable may be in a mastermind group that requires you to invest your time and money to access that kind of support. The knowledge you seek is likely being shared by someone you can choose as your mentor or hire as your coach.

Having the right people in your circles creates a level of support, accountability, inspiration, and access to wisdom that's impossible to get when you're either surrounded by the wrong people or striving in isolation. You must be willing to do what it takes to find your tribe, and as you grow and change, you have to be willing to do it again and again. Greatness does not happen in isolation. Community, accountability, and support are essential to your success. If you're looking for community, join us at iamapurposechaser.com, my Facebook community. Surround yourself with the right people.

## 26. ACCOUNTABILITY ACTIVATES ABUNDANCE

To be accountable is to be required to justify your decisions and actions. While my family members support me, they can't necessarily hold me accountable. They're too willing to accept my excuses if I fail to follow through on a plan. My husband will let me push back a deadline because he loves me. He sees me working hard, and he'll tell me it's okay to take a break. While I appreciate his compassion and kindness, sometimes what I need is a nudge and a reminder that I set my own deadline and now I need to meet it. Instead of relying on family or close friends, and then complaining that they don't hold me accountable enough, I've created a network of accountability in my life.

I believe in 360 degrees of accountability, which means I don't depend on a single source for it. Having several different accountability relationships has allowed me to remove unspoken and unfair expectations from relationships where I shouldn't expect people to hold me accountable. At the moment, I'm in two different masterminds with other business women and a mastermind for podcasters. Depending on what my goals are, I'm always in some form of coaching. My accountability partner and I also check in with each other once a quarter and each set two monthly goals for each of the Six Pillars of Wealth.

In addition to those more formal relationships, I consider my podcast my open platform for accountability. Honestly, had I not talked about pursuing my MBA in behavioral finance in an episode entitled "Impossible Means It's Not Your Priority," I might have backed out when I finally got wind of the syllabus. The workload is serious, but getting this degree is a priority for me. I've shared this goal with my entire podcast audience, and the DMs and words of encouragement they've sent me made me feel like I could do it. As I write this book, I'm pursuing my MBA.

To enjoy the full benefits of accountability in your life, employ these three types of accountability:

1. Accountability to others
2. Accountability to yourself
3. Accountability to your Creator

When author, entrepreneur, and philanthropist Nehemiah Davis and I talked on the *Redefining Wealth* podcast, he suggested creating your circle of greatness so you always have people who can lift you up. "You only grow to the extent of those that are around you," Nehemiah said. Part of your circle of greatness has to be people who are willing to hold you accountable. Your circle can provide encouragement, connection, camaraderie, support, and an element of accountability.

Many people miss the benefits of being accountable to others because they're afraid someone will steal their idea if they share it. You don't have to share your proprietary information with people, but you can't get accountability without sharing your goals with someone. Find people you trust enough to share your goals with even if you work through the details on your own. Whether it's a coach, a mastermind group, an accountability partner or some other relationship, you need someone outside of yourself who can encourage you and hold you accountable to take action on the goals you set.

Accountability to yourself starts with understanding what your values are and committing to the guiding principles by which you will live your life. You have to determine what the non-negotiables are in your life. Regardless of the circumstances, you can choose how you show up and whether or not your behavior is in alignment with your values. I took a stand years ago that I would not let people or situations dissuade me from who I say I am because there's nothing worse than breaking a promise to yourself. Failing to live up to your own values or to accomplish what you know you should have can put you in a negative spiral of self-doubt, self-rejection, and self-flagellation. Being accountable to yourself means, regardless of what's going on around you, your character doesn't change and you keep your promises to yourself.

Finally, accountability to your Creator means honoring your faith even when it's not easy, even in the face of fear and self-doubt. When you're accountable to your Creator, you do what your faith tells you to do in those difficult moments. My resilience comes from my belief that we're all called to a greater purpose. When you're accountable to a higher power, you know there's a value beyond your bank account and beyond your personal interests that you're supposed to bring to the world. You can't get stuck in your story because you recognize you have a higher purpose to fulfill.

### Redefine Wealth for Yourself

Create a plan to activate abundance by implementing each type of accountability—and follow through with it. This may include joining a mastermind group or getting an accountability partner, writing out your goals and checking in with yourself to make sure you work towards them, and getting clear on the values you'll live by regardless of what's going on in your life.

## 27. PEOPLE WANT TO SUPPORT YOU

I was speaking at a Paul Mitchell school outside of Houston once and I asked the students, "Where are my people who hate to ask for help?" One woman from my podcast audience, a Purpose Chaser, was there and shouted out, "I'd rather Google all night than ask for help." That's the case for many of us Lone Rangers. Asking for help seems like a weakness, a vulnerability, or a burden on others.

I was raised by well-meaning people to "figure it out" when I had a question or a problem. Perhaps they wanted me to develop strong critical thinking skills, but it also left me with this idea that figuring it out by myself was the only way to get anything done. Even now, I struggle with asking for support. My husband and I suffered such huge financial losses in the Great Recession partly because we waited until our backs were against the wall to ask for help. By the time we did, there wasn't much that good advice could do for us. I won't repeat that mistake. My IG handle is @seekwisdompcw because I want to remind myself every day to seek wise counsel and get support.

Today, there's nothing I attempt to do without support. When I decided I wanted to write this book, I called Candice L. Davis for help. When I'm about to do a significant media push, I call media coach TeeJ Mercer. When I'm ready to launch something new in the business, I get my team on board. I've even started asking members of my community to lend their gifts to this movement, and inevitably, someone steps up to fill the need.

My granny used to say, "Don't block people's blessings." When someone wants to give you something or help you in some way, you should let them. They genuinely want to be a blessing and be blessed in return, and you shouldn't stand in their way. Allow people to have the joy and satisfaction of supporting you.

### Redefine Wealth for Yourself
In which of the Six Pillars of Wealth—FIT, PEOPLE, SPACE, FAITH, WORK, or MONEY—are you currently struggling the most? Where do you need sound advice or support? Brainstorm where can you find that help.

## 28. ASK FOR WHAT YOU WANT

Cathy, a member of my mastermind group, worked for the same company for twenty years. Yet, she felt invisible there. With the growth she experienced and the encouragement she received in Mastery + Momentum, she started to speak up more at work. Since she started asking for what she wants, she has been consistently getting the recognition she'd long sought from her employer.

Asking for what you want and getting it isn't always a one-to-one transaction. There have been times when I've asked something of one group of people and it came to me in a completely different way. It was almost like the Universe needed to hear me acknowledge what I wanted out loud and with clarity. It wasn't for me to know or be attached to what the response looked like or where it came from. I just had to be bold in the asking.

This isn't an invitation to go around making unreasonable demands on the people in your life or to run out and ask strangers for what you want before you even build a relationship. Instead, I encourage you to learn to speak up for yourself at home, in your romantic relationships, with your children, at work, and in your business. You're already in relationship with these people, so you're in a position to ask for what you want from them. Often, giving people context, so they can understand the bigger picture, will make them much more likely to comply with your request. I've found this to be the case with my daughter. I don't mind explaining to her, even though I'm the parent, because I like having her buy-in and her willing support.

Sarita Maybin, a communications expert and author of *If You Can't Say Something Nice, What DO You Say?*, shared on my podcast that it's often more effective to make requests than it is to make demands. She suggests avoiding phrases like "You'd better do this" and instead using collaborative phrases like "Would you be willing to" and "I'd appreciate it if you would." Making the other person feel like they have a vote in what you're asking for makes it more likely that you'll get what you want. According to Sarita, these subtle changes in the way you ask for what you want can allow you to be assertive without being aggressive.

Sarita also talks about the long history of women being taught to be seen and not heard, to avoid imposing on people, and to always be polite. This programming, she says, has made many of us feel like we're out of line if we ask for something. However, her mantra is, "If you don't ask, you don't get." All too often, we want our friends, family, employers, and business partners to be mind-readers. It's extremely unfair, and when they don't somehow magically know what we want and give it to us, it only reinforces what we want to believe, that no one wants to support us anyway. Rewire that old programming and start asking for what you want.

> ### Redefine Wealth for Yourself
> Are you resentful because someone isn't giving you what you want? It could be the boss who hasn't offered you a promotion, your husband who never helps with picking up the kids, or your sister who never brings anything to your potluck dinners. Make a request—not a demand—and ask that person for what you want. Use a tone of collaboration, and when it might be helpful, give the person some context so they can understand why the request is important to you.

## 29. FIND YOUR TRIBE

On a ten-hour flight to France, I read *A Tribe Called Bliss* by Lori Harder. I'd heard Lori speak at an event, and within ten minutes of taking the stage, she'd blown my mind. I was so glad to have the opportunity to read and absorb her book, which gave me all kinds of "Get it together, girl!" vibes, on my long flight. Later, I had the chance to talk to Lori about the value of finding your tribe on my podcast and hers.

As Lori describes it, your tribe is a group of people who embrace you as you are and allow you to become more of your authentic self. If you haven't always found this kind of acceptance from your family of origin or the people you grew up with, you're not alone. Your family, friends, and the people you went to church with as a kid may have different values they want you to live up to or different ideas for how you should live your life. That's why you need to find your tribe. It may be a group of people who are already connected, or you may go about selecting people, one by one, for your tribe. You can't force friendships, but you can be intentional about bringing like-minded people into your world and creating a space in which you can give and receive.

At the same time, don't assume being in community with like-minded people will be a breeze. It still comes with challenges. In *A Tribe Called Bliss*, Lori says, "Every relationship has unspoken agreements we adhere to when we decide to form any type of bond." When something goes unspoken, it will eventually be broken, not out of malice but because anything unstated is bound to be misunderstood. Don't leave the expectations you have of each other unspoken. Share them out loud, and make sure everyone has the same understanding.

We talk about asking for help and letting people support you, but especially for high achievers, it can be hard to admit you don't know something or you're feeling weak or afraid. Being in a space with others who can identify with your struggles can make it easier for you to take off the mask and the cape and be who you are. That's one of the main reasons you need to find your tribe. For me as a businessperson, I need a community in which I can freely talk about money. I can't do that if the members of my tribe have a lot of money shame or look at my discussion of what I earn as if I'm boasting about my accomplishments.

You may be in a place where you talk with some friends about your career, others about your marriage, and still another group about your faith or how you like to spend your weekends. Some relationships will be limited to certain parts of your life, and that's okay. Keep working to find or create the community where you live your life with complete authenticity. Keep looking for your tribe.

### Redefine Wealth for Yourself

In what area of your life have you felt the least supported? What topics do you wish you had a safe space to vent about or discuss without judgment? Your tribe may be an existing group or a group of people you bring together on your own. Be intentional about looking for your perfect fit and find a place where you can be 100% you.

## 30. SEEK MENTORSHIP

When I was given a copy of *Think and Grow Rich: A Black Choice*, by Dr. Dennis Kimbro, years ago, I adopted many of the principles shared in book. In that way, Dr. Kimbro became a mentor to me. We had never met, but I applied his wise counsel. After I lost everything, and we relocated to Atlanta, one of my first jobs was as an office manager in a salon. One day, eight years after I first read his book, Dr. Kimbro walked into the salon with his wife.

When I met him, I didn't just have a fan-girl moment. I was able to speak intelligently about how his wisdom had changed my life for the better. Dr. Kimbro generously invited me to have lunch with him, and when we met, I told him my story and how I was rebuilding my finances. He encouraged me to write my first book by repurposing and adding to the blog posts I'd already written. Following his advice, I was already sixty percent of the way to writing *Real Money Answers: College Life and Beyond*, my very first book. Since then, Dr. Kimbro and I have remained in touch, and his interview on my podcast is one of the most viewed episodes on my YouTube channel.

Many of the people I consider mentors, I've never met or have only met on rare occasion. They mentor me through their books, videos, podcasts, and TV and radio shows. I recently had the honor of meeting Dave Ramsey, but he's been my mentor since I first read his book *Total Money Makeover* years ago. Michelle Obama is my mentor. Pastor Mike Todd is my mentor. I apply what they teach, and if and when we meet, I'll tell them how they've influenced me and positively impacted my life. That's mentorship from afar, and it's just as effective as personal mentorship.

I frequently hear from people who want me to mentor them. They have an idea that we'll meet for coffee once a month, I'll advise them when they have a decision to make, and they'll turn to me for career and business guidance. That's how mentorship worked in the past, especially in corporate America, but living in the information age has changed that. Knowledge and wisdom once hard to come by are readily available on the internet and in books you can download in a matter of seconds or have delivered to your house in a day or two.

The very things these people admire about me make it nearly impossible for me to take on mentees. I'm busy running a business and serving the people who pay for my coaching. I have occasionally participated in one-on-one mentoring programs, but frankly, the experience hasn't been the best for me. If you have the privilege of a formal mentorship, honor that person's investment in you. Show up for calls and meetings on time. Bring questions and challenges you want to discuss. Be humble and grateful.

If you're hoping to find a mentor, don't mourn the looming death of traditional mentorship. You can be mentored from a distance by people you may never cross paths with in real life. Just remember no mentor's advice is the final word for your life no matter how great your mentor is or what they've accomplished. If it isn't in alignment with your assignment, it's not for you.

### *Redefine Wealth for Yourself*
Choose one mentor whose work you want to study in depth. Read their books, watch their videos, listen to their podcasts, and show up for their events. Apply their advice. Get results, and when the opportunity arises, express your gratitude for what you've already learned from them.

## 31. GIVE MORE THAN YOU ASK

One day, I opened my big mouth on IG Live and shared that I was planning to hold a small event. The idea had come to me in a divine download that morning, and in my desire to be obedient, I was moving forward with it. Soon after the video aired, a young contacted me for more information. In our email exchange, she shared a lot of her story. Still a college student, she had gone through a traumatic experience and was looking for ways to use it to help people. She wanted to know the price of my event so she could save up to attend.

I sent her a message of encouragement and asked her if she'd like to volunteer for the event. "Yes, but I still need the dates and the price," she responded. I explained I was offering her an opportunity to volunteer, so she could get in the room and learn in exchange for her contribution. That way, she wouldn't have to stretch her budget or make a financial sacrifice to attend. It hadn't even occurred to her that she could be of service to me, and by doing so, create a win for both of us.

So many people look at the experts and "gurus" they admire and think they, as fans and followers, have nothing to offer these people speaking on big stages, publishing bestselling books, and running major businesses, but that's so not true. Sometimes, people in my community take the time to send me a prayer or words of encouragement via social media. They share how my work has positively impacted their lives, and they offer their spiritual or emotional support in return. It's something anyone can do, and it makes a difference. There's always something you can give.

Endeavor to create give-and-receive, not give-and-take, relationships. When you give more than you ask for, you become memorable and people are often moved to reciprocate. Sometimes, the return on your investment of giving comes in a totally unexpected way or even from an unexpected source. If you're wondering how much you have to give before you ask for something, my formula would be to give, give, and give again before you ask. Most times, you should give without asking at all. The point is to build a rapport so you're not one of the many, many people who ask way too soon. When you give from a desire to serve, people feel your sincerity. When you give from that place, you always win.

### Redefine Wealth for Yourself

Who has positively impacted you or caused you to stretch and grow in new ways? Write them a note of gratitude. Leave them a glowing review. Share that person's work, or volunteer to work their event. Give, give, and give again. It will all come back to you.

## CHAPTER 6

# Attract Allies and Advocates

S OME PEOPLE MAKE great employees, but I'm not one of them. I want change to happen faster than it typically can in a large organization. That's just a part of my entrepreneurial nature, which kept showing itself when I worked for a nonprofit during the recession. My job was to spread the organization's gospel by teaching workshops and signing people up for one-on-one financial counseling. Fortunately, one of my gifts was building relationships, so I was often invited to speak without having to be pushy. Unfortunately, I really wanted to teach my way.

I was much more effective when I delivered my own version of the curriculum than when I followed the one I was given. When I incorporated my personal stories to illustrate points, the audience responded and people signed up. My way worked, but sometimes, I was scared to follow my instincts. When representatives from other markets came to watch me present, I wanted to hold back, but my supervisor, Walter Jackson, advocated for me to do what I did best, regardless of who was watching. He argued they needed to see how I delivered the content in order to be inspired to rise to the same level.

While Walter shielded me from a lot of office politics, he and I often got on each other's nerves. We argued all the time about my fear of being fully myself. He wanted me to go for it, and he fought for me to have a chance to prove myself. Because he cleared a path for me to do things my way, I produced exceptional results in my job and eventually made the leap into something even better.

Walter, who has since passed away, was my advocate and my ally. He had my back because I showed up in a way he could believe in. I was passionate about helping people get real results in their personal finances. I was completely sold out for my belief that success with money was more than checking a few boxes on a financial to-do list. I was convinced mindset was foundational to financial success, and although it wasn't part of the official curriculum, I couldn't in good conscience skip over it.

As my direct supervisor, it would have been so much easier, and probably in his best interest, for Walter to tell me to stick to the status quo. Instead, he told me I was bigger than my job and advised me not to let it confine me. He knew I wrote for magazines and booked speaking engagements on my own time, and he encouraged me to keep going. He registered us for events where Black women were speaking, which is how I connected with the finance editor for *Essence* magazine. His support helped me develop the confidence to go out and become America's Money Maven.

When you show up and do good work, people will advocate for you when you least expect it. Walter and I were in nine-to-five jobs, but you can build allies and advocates as a freelancer, for your side hustle, or as you grow your full-time business. While most of the focus here is on professional relationships, every one of these principles can also be applied to your personal life.

## 32.  ARTICULATE THE VISION AND ENROLL OTHERS

When I was shooting the Redefining Wealth video series for my website, I needed a makeup artist. I had worked with several, but for different reasons—mostly a lack of punctuality and professionalism—I didn't go with any of them. The creative director suggested someone, and I decided to take my chances with this new person rather than rehire someone who wasn't excellent the first time. It turned out to be a great decision.

Brittany Ingram showed up early, arriving before the rest of the crew, even though she lived forty-five minutes away. From the time she started working, she was attentive and on top of things, including details that didn't fall under the responsibility of a makeup artist. She took initiative and knew her craft, so no one had to micromanage her. My experience with her was refreshing because, too often, people in her industry are more concerned with posting on social media than with taking care of their client. Brittany was the polar opposite.

On the second day of the shoot, Brittany and I talked a bit more as she did my makeup. She described her vision for her future, which included landing a full-time job as a makeup artist so she could stop freelancing. The way Brittany showed up made an impression on me, and when producers of a daytime talk show asked if I knew a reliable makeup artist they could hire, I happily referred Brittany for the position. As you've probably guessed, she got the job and realized her vision for a full-time gig.

Just as I had the power to bless Brittany with an opportunity, rest assured there's always someone watching you who has the power to bless you. When you show up ready to do good work, people will advocate for you when you least expect it. However, the only reason I was able to help Brittany execute her vision was because I knew what it was. She chose an appropriate time, after she had demonstrated value, to share her vision with me. She did so without expectation and without asking me for anything in the process.

As more people in your circles understand what you're trying to achieve, you increase your chances that someone will step in and help you get there. To enroll people in your vision, abandon the notion that it's better to keep everything to yourself. You can't expect people to advocate for you if they don't know what your vision is or can't see you working to realize it. Articulate your vision clearly and consistently without being pushy, and then go after it so your actions support your words. When it's appropriate, share your vision with mentors, colleagues, your human resources department, clients, vendors, and anyone else in your circle so they're clear about what you want to achieve. The right people will champion you when they see you putting in the work.

One note of warning: Articulate your vision, but don't expect everyone else to immediately jump on board. When I interviewed musician and creator of Beleaf in Fatherhood, Glen Henry, he explained that it wasn't his wife's responsibility to understand his vision before he brought it to fruition. "I can't blame my wife for her lack of vision when I haven't manifested anything," he said. It was his responsibility to show her his vision coming to life. Some people need proof. Articulate your vision but continue to do all you can do to execute it.

### Redefine Wealth for Yourself

Where do you see your job or business in the next three, five, and ten years? What do you ultimately want your work life to look like? Practice sharing your vision with people so you can continue to refine it and communicate it more effectively. And then get busy making it a reality they can see and invest in.

## 33. CHECK IN WHEN YOU DON'T NEED ANYTHING

Lisa Bilyeu cofounded Impact Theory, an entertainment and educational content platform, and the billion-dollar brand Quest Nutrition with her husband, Tom. She's a busy woman, but we've developed a real friendship because she makes time to check in with me for no reason at all. Her occasional calls and text messages inspire me to think of her often and to reciprocate by checking in with her. Sometimes, when I'm in a store, I'll take a picture with a Quest Bar and send it to her with a quick note to let her know she's on my mind. Lisa and I genuinely like each other and want to stay in touch however we can.

As my flight home to Atlanta landed one day, I turned off airplane mode on my phone and notifications poured in. A message from Lisa read: "Just thought of you. Getting ready to board a flight in Atlanta. Waving to you from the airport!" The message was a thoughtful surprise. I quickly texted her back and arranged to meet her near her gate before she boarded. I'll always remember that embrace: me, a tall Black woman, in the middle of the busiest airport in the world, spinning around with a tiny Greek woman, both of us thrilled to have an unexpected opportunity to cross paths. It was such a fun moment, and whenever the opportunity arises, I'm both an ally and an advocate for Lisa.

I'm sure there are people in Lisa's world who only reach out when they want something. They may send a "just checking on you" text, but a day or two later, it's followed by a request. People of influence are especially suspicious of deceptive friendliness and can see through it from a mile away. That's one of the reasons my "no" game is so strong. I've gotten used to people who only contact me when they want something, and I don't fall for it.

If a relationship really matters to you, show it. Maybe you're not close enough to text whenever you think of that person, but there are plenty of ways to build the relationship. You can share an article or book that person will find interesting or make a useful introduction. The important thing is to keep in touch without an ask attached to your communications. Don't be a nuisance. Be someone who obviously cares.

### Redefine Wealth for Yourself

Make a list of the people in your circles, starting with those closest to you. Note the people with whom you want to build stronger relationships—people who could be your allies and advocates—and devise a plan for how you'll make checking in when you don't need anything a part of your routine.

## 34. REMEMBER THE IMPORTANT STUFF

Acclaimed author, speaker, and life coach Tim Storey is a master of remembering the important stuff. Tim and I met when we appeared on a TV talk show together, but when we saw each other next, I was impressed by how much he remembered about me and my life. He mentioned several details that mattered to me, right down to my daughter's name and age. I have no idea if he keeps impeccable notes or he's gifted with a fantastic memory, but every time I talk with him, I'm delighted by how much he remembers of our previous conversations. Tim makes me feel like he cares about me and our friendship, and I sincerely want to reciprocate and support him however I can.

You can strengthen your relationships by paying attention to people and understanding what's important to them. Be a good listener and give people space to talk about themselves and their priorities. Ask questions to demonstrate sincere interest and concern. When the opportunity presents itself, ask about those things, not as a means of manipulation but because you care and want to grow the relationship. Remembering the important stuff will help you do just that.

### Redefine Wealth for Yourself

Go through your contacts and add notes to each person's listing to remind you of what's important to them. If you find you don't know much about your contacts, start paying more attention, and update those notes as you learn more about each person. Also, put birthdays and important anniversaries or events on your calendar and acknowledge them when they come up. Some of my best intel about important dates has come from social media posts, so pay attention to what you see people acknowledge and celebrate there.

## 35. MAKE SMALL THOUGHTFUL GESTURES

Winn Claybaugh, dean and co-founder of Paul Mitchell Schools, is a pro at the thoughtful gesture. Since I've known him, he has periodically sent me an orchid out the blue as a thank-you for my work with his students. When I spoke for the schools, I charged less than my normal speaking rate, but I did it because I love the students and because I love the relationship I've built with Winn. His thoughtfulness makes me feel appreciated and respected, and it nourishes our friendship.

It's great to be on the receiving end of thoughtful gestures, big or small, but one of the best ways to create allies and advocates is to be the one who makes those gestures. I make it a habit to do this in my business. I send a note of gratitude to the event organizers when I have speaking engagements and to podcast guests. Sometimes I send small gifts or treats, like my signature candle. Other times, I send a handwritten note on custom note cards designed with a drawing of me. The point isn't the cost of whatever I decide to send. The point is to demonstrate my appreciation in a meaningful way.

If you secure a deal or complete a project for someone, when someone makes a referral to help you sign a client or land a new job, when someone completes a project for you, when you hear someone has suffered a loss, or just because you think it will put a smile on that person's face—there are limitless opportunities for you to strengthen your relationships with thoughtful gestures. When they come from a good place, people recognize your positive intention and you create a lasting impression. Decide what kind of thoughtful gesture best represents you or the feeling of appreciation you have for the person you're sending it to. It might be a card, flowers, a gift basket, or a great book. Anything you do with the intention of showing appreciation, admiration, or concern will shine through as thoughtful.

### Redefine Wealth for Yourself

Think of a thoughtful gesture or two that could become your signature. Start using them right away and make them a habit by committing to either sending them out on specific occasions or to a certain number of people each month.

## 36. ALWAYS MAKE THEM LOOK GOOD

As a college intern for 92.3 FM and *The Steve Harvey Morning Show*, my job was supposed to be temporary. I had ninety days to learn as much as I could. During that time, I did my best to make a good impression, and when my tenure ended, the staff wanted me to stay. Unfortunately, they didn't have much of a budget to pay a production assistant. Rushion McDonald, who became my mentor, offered to pay the balance of my salary out of his own pocket. As an employee, I got a fair wage, my own desk, a phone line, and business cards, all a big deal to a college student.

I was so honored and humbled by Rushion's vote of confidence in me, but on my very first day as an official member of the team, I overslept. To this day, I don't know what happened. I don't oversleep. I had never shown up late for my internship. I'd been a star the whole time, and people had bent over backwards and argued on my behalf to get me the position, all for me to oversleep and show up late on my first official day. I was so embarrassed. Rushion had really gone to bat for me, and by not holding up my end, I made him look bad. It was one of the best lessons of my life. From that day forward, I'd always make the people I represent, directly or indirectly, look good.

My actions reflect on any person or organization I'm associated with, and I never forget it. When producers book me for a TV show, I give them ideas and do my best to make their job easier. They love it when I tell them I'm willing to do whatever I can to make them shine. For live events, I come earlier, stay later, and interact with the audience more than most speakers will because I want whoever booked me to receive credit and praise for bringing me on board.

When someone fights for you, advocates for you, or refers or recommends you for a position, project, or assignment, your performance reflects on that person. It's up to you to choose whether the reflection will be a positive one or not. Failing to make them look good will usually make people regret helping you. The fastest way to kill a relationship is to make someone look bad for believing in you. The best way to demonstrate your appreciation and strengthen your relationships with your advocates is to show up like a rock star and make them look like heroes for giving you the opportunity.

### Redefine Wealth for Yourself

Do you make your supervisor, boss, or company look good? If you have your own business, do you make your clients and the people who send you business look smart? Figure out how you can make your allies and advocates look good, and then do it.

## 37. HOW CAN I SUPPORT YOU?

When I worked for the nonprofit, a woman named Rhonda Williams sent me an email saying she wanted to help me in some way. She had seen me speak and really connected with my message. But I didn't know her, and honestly, my first thought was that she might be a little crazy. She didn't ask for anything, but I wondered what she could possibly want from me. It didn't dawn on me there were dozens of ways she could have helped me, like taking over administrative tasks so I could focus more of my time on creating and delivering content. I naively thought I had to be in a leadership position to benefit from support.

I forgot about the encounter until I dreamed that it was time for me to prepare to leave the organization. When I woke up, the first person I thought of was Rhonda, this woman I didn't personally know. Turned out I was the crazy one because I called her in the 7:00 a.m. hour and said, "The way you can support me is in helping me leave my job. And if you want the position, I'll train you to walk into this role, and we'll be supporting one another." I wanted to train someone to take my place when I left, and Rhonda jumped at the opportunity. From there, our relationship grew. She got the job, but she eventually came to work with me in my business, and then, after discovering her purpose in that role, she created her own career in financial education.

As much as you can give in a supporting role, what you gain is so much greater. If you're unclear about what exactly you want to do or how you want to do it, supporting someone is a great way to get a sneak peek at the inside workings of a business, organization, or event. It's a way to gain more clarity around what you want to do without going through the process of applying for jobs, investing in a new degree or bankrolling a new business. In addition, when you support someone you'd love to have as an ally and advocate, you have an opportunity to build relationships with that person and the people in their circle.

Most people in positions of power rarely hear the question: "How can I support you?" However, influential people need support just like everyone else. Not surprisingly, they're more often asked to provide the support. Imagine how it would separate you from the rest of your team if you asked your boss, "How can I support you in your goals for our team?" If you admire someone's work, imagine how you would stand out from the rest of their fans if you periodically contacted them to say, "Your work has done so much for me. How can I support you?"

If someone accepts your offer and gives you a way to lend some support, follow through and make sure you honor the request if you can. More often, when you offer support, people won't actually ask you for anything. Maybe they're like I was and don't have a clue how you could support them. Maybe there's nothing you can do for them at the moment. Whether or not they take you up on it, the fact that you offered can go a long way to building a sense of reciprocity and appreciation. Because you offered, they'll often want to do something for you in return, and even if that never happens, you'll have left them with a positive impression of you. Because you offered, you'll forever stand out from the people who are always asking.

### Redefine Wealth for Yourself

Make a list of people whose work has touched you or helped you in some way. One by one, over the next few weeks or months, reach out to each person. In your communication, briefly share how you benefited from their work. Then ask, "How can I support you?"

# 38. DON'T BURN BRIDGES

For three nights in a row, I awakened at 3:00 in the morning. Each time, I had a new realization about my former team member and her true character. But these middle-of-the-night moments weren't just about one person. The message from the Holy Spirit was clear. I needed to stop romanticizing expired relationships. I had found every reason to keep that team member on when I should have let her go. For too long, I'd justified behavior not in alignment with my values, and it was slowly being revealed to me just how badly she'd mishandled her job responsibilities. She misled clients, vendors, and team members; cost me speaking opportunities and income; and covered her tracks by blaming other people. And yet, I didn't want to burn the bridge.

I finally felt led to untie the relationship, and once I did, her gloves came off. I had seen red flags. I had witnessed how she treated other people, but I wasn't ready. In the end, she treated me with the same disrespect she'd shown so many people. She was passive-aggressive, mean-spirited, and nasty. It didn't matter how kind or professional I was in dealing with her. She gave me her true character in return, and instead of untying, she made a decision to burn the entire bridge with her antics.

Relationships never have to end with drama or hostility. You can always do your part to leave people with their dignity intact when you change the nature of a relationship or even when you end it. My mentor Rushion McDonald and I have bumped heads many times over the last twenty years. Our relationship has evolved since the time I worked directly for him, but through it all, we've maintained a mutual respect. That's the ideal in any situation.

When the radio show moved to New York, the team wanted me to come East and work with them. Instead, I left to start my own business, but Rushion and I parted on good terms. When it was time for me to go, I left the team with new systems in place, and I created a training manual to make it easier for them to on-board new interns. I also checked in with them regularly because I cared about their wellbeing.

After I lost my real estate business and ended up in Atlanta, Rushion and other people on that team helped my husband and me find work.

Imagine how that would've turned out if I had burned those bridges when I left that job. No one would have wanted to want to help me. I would've missed out on those opportunities when I needed them most. Fortunately, I represented well and left with my reputation and those relationships intact. And it has paid off for me many times over.

Most relationships either change over time or come to an end. That's a natural part of business and life, but don't burn those bridges. So many people destroy relationships without any awareness of what they're doing because they're caught up in their emotions. Whether you're the one who's changing the relationship or the other person has initiated the change, you can maintain your self-respect and help them maintain theirs. Don't discard people. If you're truly focused on building wealth, physically, mentally, spiritually, and financially, then people matter.

Burning bridges is beneath you and unnecessary, but other people may not see it that way. Be prepared for any fallout from walking away from or changing the nature of a relationship. Some people can't handle it. They'll resort to threats, extortion, drama, and gossip to punish you for "breaking up" with them. If they want to burn that bridge, there's no way you can stop them. In those instances, protect yourself, but never stoop to their level.

### Redefine Wealth for Yourself

Take an honest look at the relationships in your personal and professional life. You probably won't have to think very hard to identify any toxicity. Decide how you'll untie or change those relationships. If that change requires a conversation, have it. If not, simply adjust how and how much you interact with that person without unnecessary explanation or confrontation.

Also consider whether or not there are any past relationships you wish you'd ended on a better note. Identify what you could have done differently. Make a list of how you'll handle it better next time, and make sure you do those things in the future.

# PART III. SPACE

## Set Up Your Life to Support You

Y OUR ENVIRONMENT PLAYS a critical role in your ability to create a wealthy life. Order and organization are forms of well-being in and of themselves. They also make it easier for you to be successful with all the pillars—FIT, PEOPLE, SPACE, FAITH, WORK, and MONEY. When you design and organize your space with systems which are sustainable for you and the people with whom you share your space, you'll reap the benefits in every area of your life.

If you're like me and like most women, however, you have a demanding career and a real life, which may include people who aren't always on board with your ideas for maintaining your home, car, and office. In that case, you have to be realistic about the space you can create. The goal of the SPACE pillar isn't to create a Pinterest-ready pantry or a closet where you can take great Instagram shots. The goal is to set up systems to make your life easier and allow you to have more time to chase your purpose and create your wealthy life. And even the tidiest people have to work at it.

Don't feel obligated to apply all the principles in this section—or any of the sections. Instead, take what you need and leave the rest. Choose the strategies that speak to your natural tendencies or address your biggest issues and will give you the greatest return on your investment of time and effort. Don't worry about what anyone else might think about how you organize your space and manage your time. Set up your life to support you.

## CHAPTER 7

# Get It Together

WHEN WE ARRIVED at the SPACE pillar, my client Vivian shared that she was having challenges keeping her bedroom organized. Vivian's room was cramped and crowded with her possessions, not because she had too much stuff but because she had a roommate. She had allowed her cousin to stay with her for a couple of months, and those months had turned into a couple of years. Over that time, Vivian's room did double and triple duty for her. It was her bedroom, but it was also her home office and storage room. Because her cousin was in the spare room, Vivian's desk was next to her bed. It was uncomfortable for sleep and uncomfortable for work. She had no sanctuary in her own house. She couldn't get her environment together because she had allowed someone else to encroach on her space.

I suggested Vivian remove any extra furniture from her room. Without so many surfaces, there would be fewer places for things to pile up. She also needed to pare down her wardrobe. If clothes are bleeding out of your closet and spilling out of your drawers, you've got more than you need. These were practical steps for her to take, and they would make a real difference, but there was a bigger issue. Vivian's cluttered room was a reflection of how having her cousin live with her for so long had affected her state of mind. She had allowed this person to mistreat her by taking advantage of her generosity. Once she took the practical steps to bring order to her bedroom, she gained the strength to have the long overdue conversation with her cousin as well. The cousin moved out a few months later, and whenever I see Vivian on a Zoom call, she's sitting in her new home office.

Clutter is a physical manifestation of chaos in the mind. From the boxes stacked in your garage to random stuff shoved in your junk drawer, it's all a reflection of your mental state. Award-winning Realtor and television personality Egypt Sherrod says, "You can tell where people are in their lives by how their house looks on the inside." I agree. If you're searching for clarity in a particular area of your life, look no further than the physical representation of that issue in your environment. Cleaning up and clearing out your space will give the answers you seek an outlet to finally escape.

Eliminating clutter and bringing order to your space brings order to your life. How you create, maintain, and manage your space, contributes or detracts from your overall wellbeing. Every pillar—FIT, PEOPLE, SPACE, FAITH, WORK, and MONEY—impacts every other pillar. The spaces you live, drive, and work in all impact your health, relationships, spiritual life, professional life, and bank account, for better or for worse.

When your space is in order, it teaches you how to treat yourself and demonstrates to others how they should treat you as well. If you're the kind of person who maintains a neat and organized home, you're more than likely also the kind of person who maintains the other areas of her life as neat and organized. You have a level of respect and admiration for that woman. On the other hand, if you're the woman who trips over shoes on the way to the front door, can never find her car keys, and has more clothing on her closet floor than hanging on hangers, you're likely to treat yourself accordingly.

Organization expert Tanisha Lyons-Porter suggests you choose functional over fictional. Don't fall for the images of organization you see online or on television. "Organization is not about perfection, it's about finding systems and methods that line up with how you and your family operate," says Tanisha. Don't let social media trick you into thinking you have to model someone else's seemingly perfect organizational system. The person who posted it might not utilize that system in her real life. Organizing your home isn't about creating a post-worthy linen closet. The goal is to set yourself up to create a space that works for you and your lifestyle.

## 39. CLEAR SOMETHING SMALL

When you have a whole house to declutter, it can seem like starting small is a waste of time. But clearing the little things first will help you build the muscle to clear bigger things later. Small wins make you feel lighter and motivate you to go on to bigger projects, like your garage, basement, or storage unit. Taking care of one small area can also make it easier to get rid of things you don't necessarily connect with clutter, like toxic relationships or a job that no longer serves you.

Astrid, a member of our Facebook community who resides in London, England, sent the following note about her experience with clearing something small:

"I'd like to share that I cleared out and organised everything underneath my kitchen sink today, and I hadn't done it for 4 years. To be honest every time I went in there I was scared a spider would fall on my head! For some reason today I felt the urge to clear it out so I went with it. As I was clearing, brushing and cleaning I felt the fear fading away as I didn't see any spiders in there at all, it was just dirty and needed a clean. The lesson I got was I just need to face my fears in order for them to fade away; if I ignore them they'll just stay there. Now it's clean it has made me feel better and I won't mind going in there again."

Thin out the cabinet of coffee mugs you don't use and donate the extras. Clear a drawer or two in your office, kitchen, or bathroom. Clean out the cup-holder in your car. Get rid of all the mismatched socks cluttering your sock drawer. Starting with the small things can demystify the decluttering process and inspire you to gradually move on to bigger spaces. It can alleviate any sense of overwhelm you might be experiencing, lighten your mental load, and give you the energy you need to focus on other things. As Astrid discovered, clearing small spaces can give you big wins.

### Redefine Wealth for Yourself

Choose one very small space to clear today—a single drawer, shelf, or tabletop—and get it done. Add this practice to your daily routine until you feel ready to tackle bigger projects.

## 40. DECLUTTER WITH DISCIPLINE

When I interviewed Egypt Sherrod, she suggested tackling one room at a time by packing up everything in the room. In her process, you evaluate each item and only put back into the room what you really need or love. It's an effective strategy, but decluttering a whole room at once can overwhelm many people. If this is the case for you, then select the room you want to declutter first, and break it into sections. Work in short bursts of one or two hours at a time with scheduled breaks so you don't burn out. Once you've completed a section or a room, let that win motivate you to tackle the next one.

Crystal Escobar, author of *My Life as a Wannabe Balanced Mom*, shared on the *Redefining Wealth* podcast that she used opportunities when her husband and kids were away from home to stay behind and tackle one or two sections of her house at a time. If she tried to do the whole house, she'd have no time left for herself, but by focusing on one section at a time, she was able to enjoy some time on her own before the family came back home.

Like Crystal, I tend to tackle one project at a time. If the linen closet has gotten out of order and it's annoying me, I'll take everything out, refold it, and put it back in order. Lately, I've started involving my family in the process. It sends the message that we can either keep the linen closet the way I like it or we can spend every other Saturday redoing it together.

Decluttering in chunks is more realistic for me because I have a tendency to get sentimental about things. If I'm sorting through a box, I'll relive all the moments the items in the box represent. It's a slow process, so if there's nobody there to move me along, I can't try to take on an entire room at a time. I either need to get help or accept that going through one box will take me longer than it might take other people.

Decluttering isn't always a smooth and easy process. In our Facebook community, Shann shared that she always overestimated her time and energy and underestimated the work involved, so she ended up stressed and rushed. She had also convinced herself she couldn't do a great job at decluttering because her heart wasn't in the process. But Shann realized she went to work every day, whether she felt like it or not, and gave her job her best effort. Not *feeling* like doing something was clearly not a legitimate excuse.

Shann explained she had great self-discipline with money. She had completed a "No Spend" year, during which she didn't eat out at all. She had paid off nearly $12,000 in debt and increased her savings to $3200 on a $22,000 a year salary. (If that's not discipline, I don't know what is.) But Shann was picking and choosing where she would apply her self-discipline. The MONEY pillar got all the love while she neglected the SPACE pillar. Instead of giving up, she used her decluttering project as a starting point to develop self-discipline across all the pillars.

If you're really struggling to declutter because of a lack of self-discipline, it feels overwhelming, or your heart just isn't in it, you have options for getting the support you need. You can always hire a specialist to walk you through the process and teach you a system based on how you live. If that approach doesn't work for you, make a party of it. Invite your best girlfriends over for pizza and wine, and let them know you'll be relying on them to keep you focused, push you to make decisions, and help you sort through your clutter.

One of my girlfriends had three friends, including me, and her husband help her pack for an out-of-state move. But before we could get to the packing stage, we had to declutter. In her bedroom closet, we sorted through a massive amount of clothing she no longer loved or could no longer fit. As friends, we lent her our neutral perspective so she could honestly assess what should stay and what should go. It was a big undertaking but it made her move easier and positively affected her life. In the following months, she even lost the weight she'd wanted to lose for a while. I believe the decluttering process freed her to focus on taking care of herself so she could finally reach her weight loss goal. Declutter like you mean business and see what opens up in your life.

### Redefine Wealth for Yourself

Once you've started with the small things, decide on a larger project you can take on and commit to decluttering it. Choose one room or one section of the room. Build in twice as much time as you think you'll need so you won't feel rushed when you get down to the items that are hard to categorize. Ask for or hire help if you need it.

## 41. HIDDEN CLUTTER COUNTS

It was a lovely home, but 6500 square feet of house was much more space than we needed for the three of us. Our family spent most of our time in the same few rooms. We cuddled up together on the same sectional every night. Out of habit, we used the same bathrooms and left the others unused. It didn't make sense. There were so many things each of us wanted to do, personally and professionally, and we realized the time and money we were investing in maintaining thousands of square feet we rarely used could be much better spent on the things we really wanted. So we decided to downsize to an apartment about one-third the size of our house.

As we prepared to move from our house in Pasadena, I was shocked to find out how much clutter we had behind closed doors. I pride myself on keeping our house impeccably clean and organized, so I was convinced we had no clutter. But I discovered we had lots of things we no longer needed or wanted. It was just all neatly tucked away in cabinets and closets. We had the space to store those things, but we had no reason to keep them. It was time to let go of this hidden clutter.

We eliminated the things we no longer needed and released memorabilia for which the memories had become tainted or which no longer held the same significance. We got rid of items that brought the wrong energy to our home. As we went through the decluttering process, each of us experienced a wide range of feelings, emotionally and physically. One night, my husband told me, "This is more than decluttering. This is detoxing." He was right.

Many people hold on to objects from previous romantic relationships because they can't let go of either what they believe might have been or resentment about the way the relationship ended. One friend confided that, for over five years after they divorced, she'd kept a Ziploc bag filled with the proof that her ex-husband cheated on her with multiple women. She had moved twice, fallen in love with a new man, and in her opinion, gotten over it. But she still had the bag with her. One day, it struck her. She didn't want that old negative energy in her new home or anywhere near her new relationship. Finally, she got rid of the bag and all those reminders of dishonesty and betrayal.

If you're carrying around old love letters, pictures, or other memorabilia from previous relationships, ask yourself why you're keeping them. If you're in a new relationship or open to one, you don't need stale energy from the past. Let it go. You can also leave behind items from your current relationship that have negative energy attached to them. Every time you look at the card that came with those "I'm sorry" flowers or whatever you have with negative history attached, it puts you back in that negative place. Leave those things and the memories that go with them in the past.

Even though our clutter had been neatly stored, it had affected us and hindered our ability to create the holistically wealthy life we desired in ways we hadn't noticed. Decluttering was a means of detoxing and removing those blocks. Any kind of detox has a phase of discomfort, but even when it's painful, you stick with it because you have a goal. At the end, you come out stronger, healthier, clearer, and transformed in ways you never expected. We felt so much lighter when our clutter detox was complete, and with the move, new opportunities flowed our way.

Years ago, I recommended to a client that she clear the clutter from her home to create more space for what she wanted. When we spoke again a month later, she was excited to tell me how clutter-free her house was. I was thrilled for her and impressed she'd taken action, until she revealed she had upgraded her storage space to a bigger one and moved all her clutter there. That's not clearing the clutter. That's hiding the clutter.

Hidden, well-organized, or properly stored clutter is still clutter. Out of sight out of mind does not apply, and when you're paying for storage, as my client was, that clutter creates an unnecessary expense. It was costing me money in unneeded square footage and costing her money in storage fees. No matter where you keep it, clutter is a drain on your energy and resources. Expose and clear out your hidden clutter and free yourself of the unseen burden.

### Redefine Wealth for Yourself

Identify any hidden clutter in your life. It could be in storage units, file drawers, cabinets, closets, or drawers. It could be in the basement you rarely enter or the trunk of your car. Regardless of how neatly it's organized, if you don't need it or love it, it's clutter. As you go through the steps in this chapter, include hidden clutter in your decluttering process.

## 42. GIVE EVERYTHING A HOME

When Reagan was a baby, Gerald and I went on a date night, and his mom came over to babysit. Reagan was asleep when we returned, and we turned in without disturbing her. She woke up for a feeding a few hours later, and I went to the nursery to get her. Not wanting to turn on a light, I felt around in the dark for everything I needed. Normally, I could put my hands on diapers and wipes with my eyes closed because I had everything in its place. However, while we were out, my mother-in-law had rearranged the room. I felt so lost. She meant well, but I was tired, annoyed, and irritated, and I couldn't wait to put every item back where it belonged.

When you fail to have a place for everything and to put everything in its proper place after each use, you set yourself up for the same kind of frustration I experienced that night. When you don't have those kinds of systems in your home, you waste time and energy. One study found the average American spends two and a half days each year looking for misplaced items, like phones, glasses, keys, shoes, TV remotes, and wallets[5]. That's more than 150 days in a lifetime. As a nation, we spend $2.7 billion a year replacing things we've misplaced.

How many times have you been ready to walk out the door, only to be stalled because you can't find something you need? How often have you been late to work or to church or your children been late to school because someone in the family couldn't find their favorite shoes, last night's homework, or a lunchbox? When everything you own has a home, and you consistently put it there, you save yourself time, money, frustration, and family arguments.

Develop a habit of putting things where they belong, especially those things that are often hard to find. Install hooks or designate a bowl for house and car keys. Store the TV remote in a decorative box on the coffee table. Give each person in the house a specific place to put the shoes they wear most often. Create a space for lunchboxes, backpacks, laptop bags, and your everyday purse. Be intentional about what goes in every cabinet or drawer and explain to your family the importance of maintaining your system.

Vacation rental homes often have labels inside drawers and pictures on the interior of cabinet doors so renters know exactly where to put away kitchen utensils, cups, and plates. Especially in the beginning, you may need similar aids to make it easy for everyone to learn the system. It will take some practice before it becomes habit to put things exactly where they belong, but the improvement in the way you enjoy your space and the time and money you save will be worth the effort.

> ### *Redefine Wealth for Yourself*
> Take inventory of items in your house that are often lost, hard
> to find, or in the way. Choose a home for each of those things.
> Then, one room at a time, assess your cabinets, drawers, shelves,
> and closets. Decide what will go in each space. Reorganize
> as needed, create any reminders your family might need, and
> introduce your new system to get everyone on board.

## 43. LESS IS MORE AND SIMPLE IS BETTER

Too much furniture means to too many surfaces available for the accu-
mulation of clutter. A bed, a couple of nightstands, a dresser, and a chair
should be sufficient to furnish a bedroom. Having too many surfaces
will just tempt you to accumulate more stuff. If you put a chair in your
bedroom because you thought it would be a relaxing place to read at
night, but in fact, it's a place where you pile the outfits you try on and
discard, get rid of the chair. Move it to another room, gift it to a friend,
or sell it. It's not serving its intended purpose, and it's inviting you to
create more clutter, so it has to go.

Furniture is just one category for which less is more. I don't own an
overabundance of any one thing. I don't have fifty pairs of underwear or
socks or dozens of bras anymore. Like most people, I gravitated to my
favorites and rarely wore the others, so when I moved, I vowed no single
type of garment could ever outgrow the drawer where it was stored. I
don't need more. To make sure you have enough of every item, follow
the "rule of two" for things that will eventually wear out, like clothing.
Assess how many of each item you need for your lifestyle and then purchase two above that number.

"Less is more and simple is better" sounds like minimalism, especially when you define minimalism as consciously living with less and
prioritizing people and experiences over things. But there are no hard
and fast rules for you to follow. You don't have to meet someone else's
standard of being able to fit your whole life in a single suitcase or never

owning more than one hundred items unless that suits your lifestyle. You decide what less looks like for you. You choose what's enough, but also be realistic and recognize when you just have too much.

### Redefine Wealth for Yourself

As you clear one small space at a time or when you tackle whole rooms, keep "less is more and simple is better" in mind. Coach yourself not to keep more than you need and eliminate anything that feeds the clutter habit.

## 44. COORDINATE WHAT'S LEFT

I am the queen of coordinating, organizing every area of my home by putting like with like. Periodically, I go into the kitchen and reorganize the groceries other people have put away. In the pantry, in the refrigerator, and in cabinets, I put like items together. The only time Gatorade should be near paper towels is in the case of a spill. Those two items shouldn't sit on a pantry shelf together because drinks go with drinks and paper towels go with paper products. Grains sit next to grains. Butter and vegetables never meet until they hit the pan because dairy products go together and vegetables are stored in a different section of the refrigerator. I implement this kind of system, not just in the kitchen, but all over the house.

Because I'm a visual person and drawn to color, I organize many areas of my house by color. Having lived most of my life between California and Georgia, I don't own four seasons of clothes, so there's no need to organize my closet around seasons. Instead, I organize everything by color. My closet starts with a white section and goes all the way around to a black section. Black clothes, for example, are all hung in one section. Black hats and purses go above this section, and black shoes go below it. I even organize books by color because, when I'm looking for a book, I remember the color of the spine.

I've tried using other systems people have recommended, but they didn't work well for me. Don't get caught up trying to organize the way anyone else does it. If you need your books grouped by genre and alphabetized by author's last name, go for it. Coordinating what's left in your space should make it easier for you to find things and save you time. You can only do that with a system designed to fit the way you think and live.

### Redefine Wealth for Yourself

Once you've decluttered, it's time to create more order by coordinating what's left. If you're not sure what system will work for you, just pick one. You'll find tons of options with a quick online search. Put a system in place and live with it for a few weeks. If you find it doesn't work for you, identify why, and choose a system that addresses those issues. If it works fine but requires a little more effort than you're used to putting in, stick with it.

## 45. HIRE HELP TO MAINTAIN

The first time I hired a housekeeper, I was pregnant with my son and my doctor had ordered me on bed rest. My mom encouraged me to hire someone to help me keep my tiny, one-bedroom condo clean. I took her advice, but it wasn't something I would have thought of on my own because I grew up scrubbing baseboards with my granny. Although my grandmother living with us was like having a live-in housekeeper, we never had a paid housekeeper in my childhood home. At the time, I believed housekeepers were exclusively for rich people who lived in mansions, but once I saw the benefits, having help to maintain my home became a necessity.

Even during times when I didn't have much money, I still managed to hire help. When Reagan was little and I moved into my first house in Georgia, we hired Miss Angela to cook, clean, and take care of Reagan while I worked or traveled. I couldn't afford her help, but we boarded her and bartered with her. She had another gig, and we got an inexpensive car for her so she would have transportation.

We always manage to figure out how to get help around the house. When we hired Miss Angela, I *felt* like we couldn't afford it because I was just getting my post-recession business off the ground. But I *knew* we couldn't afford to function without support. The time I would have taken to go to the grocery store, scrub toilets and mop floors, prepare every meal, and run errands was time I used instead to build my business. I chose to make it work so I could focus that time on growing my business and perfecting my craft.

When it comes to hiring help, you have to look at the bigger picture. I've heard women say they could never hire a housekeeper "because no one scrubs floors like I do." But you're not in the floor-scrubbing business. Scrubbing floors is not your purpose. If you must do the floors your way, hire someone to help you and touch up the details the way you want them after the housekeeper leaves. Even if you enjoy aspects of cleaning, taking on regular housecleaning as your personal obligation is a time-consuming habit. Pick a thing or two you really like to do and hire someone to do the rest, or simply invest in a housekeeper who comes a little less often. You can't complain that you don't have time to start a business or get regular exercise if you're unwilling to allow someone else to take up the slack and give you the time.

Look at it this way. If you have the potential to create $10,000 or $100,000 in your business or your career, then the $100 a week you pay someone to help you maintain your space is an investment in making that potential your reality. What a housekeeper or cleaning service does in three hours would likely take you six, nine, or twelve hours to finish. If you've prioritized regular exercise or time with your family, house-keeping help will free up space in your calendar for you to focus on those things. Don't let an overdeveloped sense of pride in doing everything yourself or a belief that it's just too expensive keep you from hiring help to maintain your space. You do not have to do it all, and there's always a way to afford help. It's not a luxury. It's a necessity.

### *Redefine Wealth for Yourself*

If you have the means, hire someone to come in as often as you need to help you maintain your space. If you're not sure how you can afford it, examine your budget for funds you can allocate to this priority or get creative about ways you can barter for housekeeping services.

## CHAPTER 8

# Add the Energy You Want

WHEN I BOUGHT a duplex so my mom could live in one unit, I longed to give her a greater sense of peace and a space in which she could focus and rest. My childhood home was a two-bedroom apartment, and as an immigrant family, we often welcomed relatives to stay with us. At any given time, there could be up to ten people sleeping in those two bedrooms. We all shared one bathroom, and we washed our clothes at a laundromat across the street. Our home was always cluttered because, as people came and went, my mom would hold on to things for them. I wanted her to experience a clutter-free, harmonious space that supported and energized her, a space where her wellbeing came first. As I write this, she has lived there nearly three years and her home is still organized and peaceful.

Not long after she moved into her new home, my mom broke her shoulder in a car accident. Fortunately, we were able to bring in a hospital bed so she could be comfortable at home while she recuperated. "I'm so grateful for this space," she told me, "because I wouldn't have been able to do this at my old place." There was too much stuff in her previous home. A hospital bed would never have fit. Without the clutter, she could have whatever she needed to be safe and well cared for, and she welcomed visitors, knowing they'd be comfortable in her home.

When my mom walks into her home, she's greeted by a gallery wall decorated with pictures of her descendants. My brother and I are in the middle, and her grandchildren surround us. A small table holds pictures of her great-grandchildren. In her old home, she never had anything like this simple display of her loved ones, and it makes her smile. While my mom was never big on candles, I also put candles all around her home, and over time, she has used them and replaced them. These inexpensive touches add a sense of love and warmth to her space.

My mom's home is her sanctuary. She has maintained the level of organization and simplicity we created when she first moved in because she likes living this way. She could easily have reverted to the way she used to live, but she hasn't, and every time we visit her, one of us remarks on how good it feels to be in her space. It's the kind of home where you get so comfortable it's easy to find yourself taking an unplanned nap. It's a place we all enjoy.

Once you've decluttered your space and organized what you've decided to keep, you have a clean slate to create the energy you want. Your home, in particular, should be a sacred space for you and the people who live with you. The spaces you spend the most time in will both reflect and influence your energy. If you're frazzled and indecisive, your home will likely be disorganized and uncomfortable. If your home is tranquil and comfortable, you're likely to feel focused and at ease. Don't compromise the energy in your space. Add the energy you want to the spaces that matter most.

## 46. CREATE YOUR MONEY-MAKING SPACE

One day, I looked around my home office and realized it didn't look like the space of a six-figure business owner. I was just starting over and had grabbed whatever space I could for my business. Somehow I ended up sharing my space with a lot of things that weren't income producing and could easily become distractions, including an ironing board, the unfolded laundry, and a treadmill. I wasn't earning six-figures yet, but I wanted my space to reflect what I was trying to create. I needed a desk that looked like someone could sit there and write a bestselling book.

My office wasn't the space of a woman committed to becoming a successful business owner. I worked every day in the environment of a woman who treated her business like a hobby. There was a chance she could be successful, but the odds were against her. I had to claim that room as my money-making office space and get my family on board with the fact that this was no longer the spare room. This was my office, and it was to be treated as such. I removed everything that could distract me from my purpose, and I brought in elements to inspire and motivate me.

Whether you work at a table in your home or a desk in an office space, your work area should reflect that it's your money-making space. If you work in a shared office, your design may be limited by office rules, but do what you can to make even the smallest cubicle feel like your money-making space. If you're starting a business from home, creating a home office may mean taking over a spare room, a guest room, or a storage space. Working in a room that serves multiple purposes can keep you straddling the fence and prevent you from fully committing to your business, so carve out an area just for business. Wherever you work, be clear and intentional about designing it as your money-making space. This is where your career or your business will grow to create the income goals you set for yourself.

Once you choose a dedicated money-making space, clear it of anything that doesn't serve your purpose. Then, take the time to add the energy you want with design elements that inspire, motivate, and encourage you. Hang a vision board or other reminders of your goals. Decorate with motivational quotes and inspirational reminders of the wealthy life you're creating. Post your project plans, calendars, or to-do lists where they can get your attention every day. Create a space that makes it easy to step into your purpose and earn money every day.

*__Redefine Wealth for Yourself__*
Take a look around your work environment. Does it reflect who you are becoming? Whether you work for yourself, someone else, or both, set up your money-making space to support you in earning the income you say you want to earn.

# 47. MAKE YOUR HOME YOUR SANCTUARY

It gave me so much satisfaction to help my mother make her new home a tranquil space. It changed her life for the better, but that story isn't unique to our family. I often hear from women in the Facebook community who experience dramatic shifts when they put some time and effort into creating a supportive space. (Join us at iamapurposechaser.com.) Aylin Öztemur, a Purpose Chaser who lives in Germany, shared that she too had transformed her home into a sanctuary after listening to the *Redefining Wealth* podcast. Aylin wrote me to say, "A few weeks ago I listened to your podcast with the professional organizer, which truly inspired me to reorganize my space and declutter everything. As a result, I feel so much more relaxed and clear on my thoughts. I find myself having more time for things that matter to me and only bring me joy."

The original meaning of sanctuary is sacred space. Your behavior in the community center, classrooms, and hallways of a church tends to be more relaxed and casual than your behavior when you enter the actual sanctuary. There, you take on a different demeanor. It's a space that deserves a higher level of respect, and regardless of the conversation you were having or how angry or annoyed you were before you got there, when you walk into the sanctuary, you leave all that behind. The reverence you have for that space causes you to change your energy. Your home deserves a similar level of respect.

A sanctuary is a place of safety and refuge, a place of relaxation and joy. When your home becomes your sanctuary, it's the one place in the world you can always go for peace and comfort. It's the place where you feel most supported and secure. It's a space that nourishes your creativity and your mental clarity, and it sets the stage for how you and your family will function at home and in the world.

If coming home from a trip or after a long day makes you feel peace and joy, your home is probably already your sanctuary. However, if coming home leaves you feeling irritated or anxious, you may have some work to do in this area. Identify the specific things that detract from your enjoyment of your home. It's hard to experience tranquility and security in a cluttered, disorganized, or less-than-clean space. If you've implemented the suggestions in Chapter 7, you've laid a good foundation for making your home your sanctuary.

### Redefine Wealth for Yourself

Begin to treat your home as a sanctuary. Set boundaries for the people, things, and behaviors you will allow within the walls of your home, permitting only those that honor your space.

## 48. CREATE YOUR SIGNATURE SCENT WITH CANDLES OR FLOWERS

When Brittany, the makeup artist I mentioned in Chapter 6, gifted me with candles named after Leimert Park, where I grew up, I had no idea they'd lead me to my signature scent. When the candle maker, Alexandria Greenwood of Intuition.LA, hand-delivered them to my house, she and I discovered we'd gone to the same high school. We instantly hit it off, and I loved the Leimert Park candles so much that I ordered more right away. I put them all over my house to help create the ambience I wanted for holiday season.

In the following weeks, I realized how much the scent positively influenced the energy in my home, and I decided to have Alex create a custom scent for me. I really enjoyed her candles, but I also wanted something that fully represented me. I wanted a scent that evoked a sense of peace, and over the course of several days, I experimented with various scents. Once I narrowed down my favorites, Alex and I worked together to craft my custom scent, something that smells like I want to feel every day. Now, I burn Peace by Patrice candles all over my home. I've also made them available for purchase at PeacebyPatrice.com so anyone who wants tranquility in their home can invoke the feeling with my signature scent.

Scent has become a part of my rituals, setting the tone for specific moments. I often light a candle before a coaching session, during my prayer time, or when I'm working on special projects. The smell of the candle puts me in the frame of mind to hold space for my coaching clients, connect with God, or focus on the project at hand. I even take a candle with me when I check into a hotel for a working weekend.

We often forget how much smell affects the mood and energy of a space, but emotions and aromas are often connected. Most of us link specific smells to some of our best childhood memories, like baking your favorite cookies or the aroma of freshly cut grass on a summer day. Your signature scent can evoke pleasant feelings for you now and be tied to pleasant memories in the future.

### Redefine Wealth for Yourself

Take the time to discover the scents that evoke the energy you want in your home. Try candles, fresh flowers, and essential oil diffusers until you find something you like enough to make it your signature scent.

## 49. BUILD YOUR LIFE'S PLAYLIST

Music has always been a part of my daily life, but over the years, I've learned to use it more productively. In middle school, I tried to listen to Tupac and Biggie while I studied, but I soon realized the lyrics were too distracting for me. I ended up typing the words I heard because I didn't have the capacity to listen to lyrics and study at the same time. By high school, I switched to instrumental music as my study soundtrack. Listening to the jazz instrumental versions of hit songs helped me focus and concentrate on my work.

These days, our house is typically filled with music, and many of our family memories are underscored by the music of the moment. From Halloween until our wedding anniversary on December 29th, Gerald has Christmas carols on rotation. During the day, when we're working, we play instrumental music. On the weekends, my husband will blast R&B or gospel, and if he wants to be the cool dad, he'll get a little ratchet with his music selection during our Saturday clean-up time.

Music is a part of how we live. It helps us create the energy and atmosphere we want in our home at any given time. I also use music to set the tone for work when I'm away from home. When I held a retreat for Mastery + Momentum, I set up to welcome the women with flickering Peace by Patrice candles and a praise-and-worship playlist. I was creating a sense of calm, but one of my team members had a run-in with the hotel staff and came in ready to fight. She was messing up the vibe, and when I told her so, she explained she'd woken up listening to DMX, so she was in a fighting mood. She and I were in very different head spaces because of the music we'd listened to as we prepared for the retreat.

Music can get you hyped for your workout or ready to take on a big project, or it can tap into your angry side. It can make you happy, or it can make you dwell on everything that's ever gone wrong in your life. If you don't believe music has the ability to alter your mood, pay attention to your favorite movies. Directors use music to create atmosphere and elicit the desired emotional response from the audience. Whether you're aware of it or not, the music you allow in your space can affect you for better or worse.

When you're building the playlist for your life, don't limit yourself to music. The right environmental sounds can also help you create the energy you want in your home. Gerald often puts on aquarium sounds in our living room during the day, and we let ocean sounds play while we sleep. Create the energy you want—peaceful, upbeat, soothing, or joyful—by choosing the soundtrack of your home.

***Redefine Wealth for Yourself***
Make note of how different artists, genres, songs, and sound-scapes affect your mood. Become selective about the sounds you allow in your space, and choose those that best serve you.

## 50. ELIMINATE THE ENERGY DRAINS

Many years ago, I read *Coach Yourself to Success* by life coach Talane Miedaner, and she suggested writing down everything that drains your energy. I walked through my home, room by room, and I created a master list of everything in my environment that irritated or annoyed me. The process allowed me to get all those annoyances out of my head, where they caused a constant drain on my energy. Once I had them on paper, those tasks had a sense of urgency for me. The master list made it easier to eliminate those annoyances, one by one, and as I made progress, my confidence grew and my energy felt replenished.

All the things you've been meaning to do but haven't gotten to drain your energy every time you see them. They remind you that you're failing to create the life you say you want to live, which chips away at your confidence. Each irritation is a reminder that you don't keep your promises to yourself. Every time you complain or frown because you still haven't replaced the button on the jacket you really want to wear or the garage door still makes a weird sound, it messes with your energy. Just as harmful, if someone else is responsible for the undone task, it can have a constant negative impact on your relationship with that person.

That annoyance, irritation, or frustration may seem like it's not a big deal because, after all, these are often small things, but those negative thoughts affect you. They're detrimental to your body, mind, and spirit. That's why I write my master list every year. It's the nudge I need to get to work and take care of small tasks that have lingered in my life. As I accomplish each one, a little more weight is lifted and my energy is replenished. Nip those energy drains in the bud so you can protect your space and create the energy you want.

### Redefine Wealth for Yourself

Walk through your home, room by room, area by area, and identify the small tasks that have gone undone. No item is too big or too small to make the list. Identify a time each day or each week when you'll handle a few of those tasks. Don't worry about how long the list is or how long it takes you to complete it. As long as you make consistent progress, you'll eliminate those energy drains. Repeat this process at least once a year.

## 51. BRING IN TOUCHES OF BEAUTY

When I was at my lowest point financially, and I found a $50 Target gift card someone had given us as a baby gift. I could've done a lot of things with that money. Our family of three had just relocated from Los Angeles to Louisiana after losing our business, our home, and most of our worldly possessions. My husband and I were struggling to find work, and every dollar counted. I could've used the gift card to buy food, diapers, or toiletries. But I made a different choice.

Instead of spending the money on more practical necessities, I went to the clearance section for home goods. I found red and black towels and a black-and-white shower curtain. I bought a rug and one of the rug-like toilet seat covers everyone used to have for some reason I can't quite understand now. I also purchased a red bowl where we could keep our toiletries, since the tiny bathroom in our six hundred-square-foot apartment had very little storage space. I needed that touch of beauty and organization so much that I was willing to make sacrifices in other areas of my life to have it.

In the time that we lived in that apartment, the bathroom became a sacred space for me. I didn't have room in my home for a prayer closet, so I secluded myself in the bathroom when I needed to be alone with God. Because I'd made it an appealing space, on my very limited budget, it felt good to be in there. It became a place where I could escape during a stressful, tumultuous time. That's where I had the crying-on-the-floor moment that changed my life and set the direction for my new business. My epiphany couldn't have happened in a disorganized, unattractive space because I would never have been in there long enough to hear from God. In the end, that $50 was well invested.

Bringing touches of beauty into your space will affect the energy in positive ways. Beauty can uplift, comfort, and inspire, and as my experience proves, you don't have to invest a lot of money to beautify to your home. Start where your budget allows, and in whatever ways you can, make your space appealing to you.

### Redefine Wealth for Yourself

Add touches of beauty to your home by choosing design elements that appeal to your personal aesthetic. From throw pillows to wall hangings or curtains, make each room in your home a space you find beautiful.

## 52. HANG SOMETHING THAT MAKES YOU SMILE

I first got into affirmations in my twenties, and during that time, I created a vision board filled with words that affirmed me, my belief in myself, and my ability to create the life I wanted. My vision board also included a card my dad gave me when I was twelve years old and a card on which a mentor had written a lovely note, praising me for the kind of young woman I was becoming. A handwritten note my mother had given me in high school also made the board, as did quotes that inspired me. The board even had a cover of *Think and Grow Rich: A Black Choice* by Dr. Dennis Kimbro, who served as my mentor years later after our chance meeting.

I hung my vision board where I'd see it every day as I walked out the door, and each time I passed it, I paused for just a few seconds to take it in. That brief moment helped me set my expectation for the kind of day I was going to have. Every single thing on that board created positive thoughts about me, my relationships, and my potential. It has since hung in closets and been stored in basements, but I still have it.

My vision board was what I needed at that time in my life. It was the one thing I hung on my walls that I could count on to make me smile. Today, a painting my husband and I bought on a trip to Cuba hangs in our home. Every time I look at it, the painting reminds me of a lovely time with my husband and the fun we had with the other couples who traveled with us. It's one thing I can count on to make me smile, and when I see it every day, it's a guaranteed energy booster.

### Redefine Wealth for Yourself

Look around your home and assess how the decor on your walls makes you feel. If nothing makes you smile, decide what you'd like to look at every day and hang it where you can't miss it.

**CHAPTER 9**

# Timing Is Everything

O N AVERAGE, AMERICANS spend more than four hours a day watching TV and more than three hours each day on their smart phones.[6] In 2019, the average adult who used the internet spent almost two and a half hours a day on social networks.[7] At the same time, people constantly complain that they're too busy to get fit, too busy to spend quality time with their loved ones, too busy to start a business, or too busy to develop the necessary skills to advance their career. Looking at the statistics, it seems most people have a serious lack of awareness of how much time they have and how they spend it.

In most cases, "too busy" is just an excuse—and not a very good one—to avoid doing hard things. Ultimately, you and I have the same twenty-four hours in each day as former first lady Michelle Obama, media mogul Oprah Winfrey, and founder of Salamander Hotels and Resorts, Sheila Johnson. Your week consists of the same 168 hours they all get in a week. These women may look busy, but my guess is they've accomplished all they have by being intentional with how they use their time.

A lack of time is rarely the real reason you don't get things done. It's much more likely that you need to learn to manage your time in new ways. When you learn how to protect your time, you'll find you have all the hours you need to work out, start your business, write your book, pursue a degree, or go after any other goals you've set for yourself. It comes down to this: *if a goal is a priority for you, then you will make time for it.* Sometimes a goal sounds good to you, but you just never seem to get to it. You're interested, but you're not committed. When you're fully committed, you're willing to learn to manage your time effectively, even when it means giving up some of the activities that consume your time and keep you too busy to accomplish your goal.

Because I share so much of my life with my community, Purpose Chasers often ask me how I get so much done, and my answer is always the same. It boils down to prioritizing my time and using it effectively, skills I've developed and refined over years of practice. The principles in this chapter will show you exactly how I manage to run my business, spend time with my family, and take care of my physical, mental, and spiritual wellbeing without feeling like I never have enough time.

## 53. SIMPLIFY YOUR SCHEDULE

Effective time management didn't always come naturally to me. In fact, I used to be one of those people hustling and grinding and cramming as much as possible into every day. I thought doing more and staying busy with work was the best way to maximize my time. Back then, I was so focused on building my business that I allowed it to take over my life. I didn't make time for the other things I said mattered to me. I needed more time to take care of me, to hang out with my family, and to practice my faith.

Just doing more wasn't serving me, so I decided to take a different approach and simplify my schedule. I started by blocking days for specific kinds of work or activities. Instead of using my whole Saturday to take care of myself and missing out on time with my family, I made Wednesdays all about me. On Wednesdays, I matter most. I get my hair and nails done, go to therapy, and focus on personal and professional development, and if I'm in school, I do my schoolwork. On Tuesdays, content matters most, and I record podcast episodes and create other content for my business. Each day has a theme that allows me to focus without distraction. Batching like tasks and projects on the same day is an essential strategy to simplify your schedule.

Another essential strategy is to say no to requests that don't serve you. Dr. Mildred Peyton, shared the following about the power of saying no. "My time management improved tremendously once I became part of the Purpose Chaser community. After listening to one of Patrice's podcast about being okay with saying no, it allowed me to manage my time better by eliminating activities or requests by others that don't support my goals or obligations at the time. Having this confirmation gave me more confidence without feeling guilty for putting myself first."

Other people will always want to leverage your time to meet their own goals, but you get to decide when that works for you and when it doesn't. If you're giving away too much of your time to people and organizations, you'll have to let something go to have the time you need to chase your purpose. You'll have to learn to say no—or back out after saying yes—so your schedule isn't overcomplicated by other people's needs.

Let me be clear, even though I'm going to make a lot of pastors mad. Saying no to simplify your schedule includes saying no to church commitments. If your schedule is packed with the usher board, marriage ministry, choir rehearsal, and teaching Sunday school, but you don't have time to go to the gym or have date night with your spouse, I highly suggest you start saying no at church so you can say yes to your other needs. Give someone else the opportunity to serve, and go create more harmony in your life.

Finding the right balance for your daily, weekly, and monthly schedule takes some practice, but it's worth the effort. Let go of obligations that no longer serve you. Keep simplifying your schedule by getting clear about what you're willing to take on and by batching like tasks. Over time, these practices will become second nature and make managing your time much less stressful.

*Redefine Wealth for Yourself*
Examine your weekly schedule and assess where you spend your
time. Where you can, group similar tasks on the same day, and
eliminate obligations that no longer serve you.

## 54. STOP MULTITASKING

In *Exponential Living*, empowerment speaker and life strategist Sheri
Riley writes that, instead of trying to multitask, we should focus on
maximizing our time and efforts. I couldn't agree more. The concept of
multitasking, as we usually think of it, is a myth. Your conscious brain
can't focus on two or more tasks at a time. If you try to multitask, your
brain has to switch back and forth between each task, and each time
it makes the switch, there's a lag time before you get focused again. If
you have a task to complete, it's much more effective to get one job done
before you dive into the next thing.

When you try to write an email and talk on the phone at the same
time, for example, you aren't focused on both tasks at once. You're switching back and forth between the two, so you're likely to miss parts of the
conversation or type in your email the words you meant to say to the
caller. No one is a master multitasker. The human brain doesn't work
that way. Don't delude yourself into thinking you're an exception to this
rule by setting yourself up to do several things at once.

It's also easy to unintentionally build multitasking into your day by
leaving yourself open to distractions. Your brain is constantly looking for
what's important now, so if you have notifications for text messages, DMs,
social media posts, and emails going off all day, you feel drawn to check
your phone every time you hear it buzz or ding. For the past six years, I've
had no notifications on my phone. I check my messages when I decide it's
time to check them, not on somebody else's schedule. This allows me to
stay focused on the task at hand and finish it much more quickly.

You know when someone isn't giving you their full attention in a
conversation. You keep repeating yourself and checking to see if they're

following you. Because that person is doing multiple things at once, you feel like your conversation isn't a priority. In the same way, when you attempt to multitask, you treat the task at hand like it's not really a priority for you. Challenge yourself to reduce the multitasking in your day so you can focus on the things that matter most and get more done. Stop multitasking so you can make the most of your time.

> **Redefine Wealth for Yourself**
> Silence all the unnecessary notifications on your phone and choose when you'll check email and other messages. Train yourself to bring a task to completion before starting on the next thing or giving in to distractions.

## 55. CALENDAR EVERYTHING

When I introduce the concept of calendaring in Mastery + Momentum, there's no shortage of grumbling from the women in the group. There's a collective sigh when they realize calendaring is an essential part of what they've signed up for with the mastermind. They believe they're already too stressed and busy and don't have time to put everything on a calendar. However much they complain, I advise them to put everything that matters on their calendar before the week begins.

Most people respond to the concept of calendaring their time the same way they respond to budgeting their money. They have a fear of anything written down because they feel restricted, like they're being told what to do. But just like you create your own budget, you also manage your own calendar. At the end of the day, you're the only one in control of how you spend your money and how you spend your time. The only person telling you what to do is you.

Your calendar is a tool to help you achieve what you say you want to achieve. Just as your budget identifies where you choose to spend your money, your calendar makes clear where you choose to spend your time.

It's a reminder to yourself to stick to the plan and do what you said mattered most. Rather than getting mad when the notification goes off to remind you of your next task, remember this is what you decided in advance you wanted to do.

Money expert Dave Ramsey says that when creating your budget, you should give every dollar a name. So if you have $5000 income for the month, your budget should account for where all $5000 will go. When it comes to your time, I suggest you give every 15-minute block of time a name. Some things may require several blocks, but other tasks can be completed in just a few minutes if you focus.

Your time is a finite resource, so you can't just keep packing things on the calendar. Once your calendar is filled for the week, you can't add a task or commitment without taking that time from something else. Recognizing this will force you to prioritize because, in the end, some things just won't make the calendar. You get to decide what's important enough to get some of your precious time.

Over the years, I've developed a process to make my calendar work for me. On Saturday or Sunday, I look at the week ahead. I start by creating affirmations about what I want to accomplish and reminders about how I want to think about my week. Then, I choose the three big things I want to accomplish. I learned to create a priority list like this, instead of a to-do list, from Tanya Dalton's *The Joy of Missing Out.* If I accomplish those three things, I can look back over my week and know I accomplished the things that mattered.

Next, I block time on my digital planner to accomplish my three big items. When I get down to daily planning, I switch to paper, where I record the specific tasks I'll complete to accomplish those goals. At one point, I used a different color for each of the Six Pillars of Wealth, but in my desire to simplify, I cut back to three colors for work, personal, and travel. With a glance, I can see, if my whole calendar is purple, I'm probably working too much. If there's a lot of green, I need to take a break from travel. If you're a visual person, color-coding may work well for you.

I also remain flexible. If something has to change in my day, I edit the calendar accordingly and move tasks to the next available time block. If

I'm in a flow with writing or creating content, I may choose not to stop when the time block ends. If so, I'll take a moment to adjust my calendar to stay with the project a little longer.

Remember to put some grace in your day. People run late. Meetings run over. You need time to transition between tasks, to refuel and refresh. If you expect a meeting to take forty-five minutes, schedule a fifteen-minute buffer so you can take care of your basic needs between appointments. Make the most of your time, but don't sacrifice all the other pillars on the altar of WORK, or any one pillar, when you're filling in your calendar for the week.

You don't have to use my system of planning to manage your time. For some people, two calendars will be one too many. Other people have a strong preference for paper or need the reminders they can only get from a digital calendar. You get to decide what works for you. Experiment, and remember your calendaring process isn't set in stone. It can and will change based on your changing lifestyle and needs.

### Redefine Wealth for Yourself

Your attitude will determine the level of success you have with calendaring, so embrace the concept. If you're not using a calendar yet, choose paper or digital, whichever you think will work best for you, and take time to plan the coming week. Decide in advance how you want to spend your most valuable resource.

## 56. TIME YOUR TASKS

Early in our relationship, Gerald would wake up early on Saturday mornings to quickly get chores done around the house so he could get out in those streets and see what was happening in the world. I didn't want to wake up at 7:00 and spend the next two hours cleaning, and I really believed I needed that much time to complete weekly chores. I grew up with a Belizean granny, and I learned if you do something, you do it all the way. There was no such thing as a quick clean-up. Our cleaning was long-suffering. The floors had to sparkle, and the baseboards had to shine. Gerald, on the other hand, liked things neat and clean, but he didn't see a reason to get down on his knees and scrub every corner.

We solved our conflict with fifteen-minute cleaning blitzes. Gerald set a kitchen timer. Reagan sat in her bouncy seat and watched as we tackled a room until time was up and we zipped to the next one. I was surprised to discover how much we could do in that short period. The job was done well enough to satisfy both of us without committing the whole morning to the process. There might have been a little dust on the baseboards, but I learned to let it go.

Most tasks don't have to take as long as they do. According to Parkinson's Law, work expands to fill the time available. Human nature is to take every bit of the time allotted to complete a task or project, and often, we take even longer. A project you could complete in a month will expand to take six months if you let it. But we don't work weeks and months at a time. We work minutes and hours at a time. A project expands to six months because tasks you could have completed in an hour take three or six hours. When you give yourself two hours to clean the house, you'll find ways to fill all one hundred twenty minutes. If you only give yourself an hour, remarkably, you'll still finish with a clean house.

Apply Parkinson's Law in your personal and professional life by allowing yourself the minimum required time to complete any given task. Timing your tasks will show you some tasks actually don't take as much time as you thought. Consciously choose how much time you want to dedicate to any given activity so you can spend more of your time on the things that matter most to you.

### Redefine Wealth for Yourself
When you take on any routine task, set a timer for how long you believe it should take. Commit to completing the task within the time you set.

## 57. THE PARADOXES OF PROXIMITY AND FAMILIARITY

When we moved back to Atlanta, I was happy to find a church right down the street from our home that was a good fit for us. I imagined waking up on Sunday mornings, enjoying a leisurely breakfast with my family, and arriving at church with plenty of time to spare. However, it didn't exactly turn out that way. Instead, we were constantly late for service. People who lived almost an hour away arrived for we did, and week after week, we ended up in the overflow parking lot. I finally realized we were falling victim to the paradox of proximity. Because the destination was so close, we were more likely to arrive late. We took for granted that we had more than enough time to get there and then gave ourselves less time than we needed.

The paradox of proximity isn't the only flawed thinking that can make you consistently late. The paradox of familiarity can also become a problem. When your destination becomes a part of your routine, you start to think you don't need as much time to get there. When you have to drive to a new place, you probably give yourself plenty of extra time in case you miss a turn, your GPS needs to recalculate one too many times, or there's more traffic than you anticipated. However, because you know the route to work or your kid's school, you start to believe you can get there quickly no matter how far away it is. You leave yourself just enough time to get to the familiar place, and when you arrive, you're actually surprised to find you're late.

Arriving late can be a stressor for you and for anyone who's waiting for you to get there. It can also inconvenience other people by throwing off the schedule. Arriving late to a doctor's appointment, for example, could mean every patient after you has to wait unnecessarily. You don't need that stress, and neither do the people waiting for you to arrive. If you're going somewhere close by or somewhere you've been a hundred times, don't underestimate the time it will take you to get there. Overcome the paradox of proximity or familiarity by giving yourself a little more time than you think you'll need.

> **_Redefine Wealth for Yourself_**
> If you have a problem arriving on time, even though your desti-
> nation isn't far, time exactly how long it takes you to get ready
> and travel from doorstep to doorstep. Then add a few minutes
> to that time to make sure you're never late again.

## 58. REBUKE "ONE LAST THING"

It was almost time for me to leave my home office and pick up Reagan
from school. I looked at the clock and thought about how short the drive
was (darn paradox of proximity), and I decided to send one more email
before I left to get her. It would just take a couple of minutes, I thought.
That way, when we got home, I could put work aside and focus on being
with her. Convinced this was the smart plan, I took a few minutes to
compose the email. Then, I read it over and gave it a bit more thought.
Finally, I proofread it, pressed send, and dashed out of the house ten
minutes after I should've been pulling out of the driveway. When I arrived,
the carpool line was empty and Reagan was one of the last kids there.

Doing one last thing before I left to pick up my daughter made me
late again and again. Reagan didn't like standing there every day, wondering when I'd arrive, while her friends drove away with their parents.
I said my relationship with her was a priority, but I wasn't treating it
like one. Once I realized how I was making her feel, however, I had to
admit I wasn't managing my time well. I decided to rebuke the notion
of doing one last thing and give myself the time I needed to pick her up
without making her wait.

Back then, I was consistently late for appointments because, in an
effort to make the most of my time, I'd developed a habit of squeezing
in every possible task and leaving at the last possible minute. If you
find yourself in the same position, make a decision to rebuke one last
thing. Become hyper-aware of where you need to be, when you need to
be there, and how much time it really takes you to get dressed, gather
your things, get in the car, and make the drive. Stop trying to do one

last thing before you go. In doing so, you choose to honor other people's time and your own.

> **Redefine Wealth for Yourself**
> Whenever you find yourself thinking, "Just one last thing, and then I'll leave," let the thought trigger you to put down what you're doing and go. Develop a habit of giving yourself a little more time than you need to get there instead of cutting it close.

## 59. ASK YOURSELF, "WHAT REALLY MATTERS TODAY?"

Every morning, at eight o'clock, an alert goes off on my phone. It says simply: "What matters today?" This is my daily reminder to think about the Six Pillars of Wealth and focus on what I choose to prioritize. This can be a struggle for me because my natural tendency is to be an over-achiever. I used to live under the burden of superwoman syndrome, believing I should be able to do all things, but I've learned to be more discriminating about what's important enough to get my time. For me, this means focusing on my three big things for the week and all the actions I need to take to get them done.

Whether you're a homemaker, a working mom, a single professional, a business owner, or you balance some combination of those roles, there's no limit to what could take up your time. In your home, there's always something you can clean, organize, shop for, or fix. On your job, there's always something your boss would love to have you do. In your business, there's always a new project you can take on or strategy you can test. Something else can always be done, but it can't all be done in one day. When you decide what matters in advance, you run a much lower risk of falling for distractions.

When you're chasing purpose you have to focus on what's important now. Depending on your priorities, that might mean reading every day with your child while the laundry waits. It might mean working on the first product for the business you want to launch and answering emails later. Remember some things are important but aren't urgent. Define for yourself what really matters today so the day doesn't decide for you.

### Redefine Wealth for Yourself
Before you start each day, ask yourself, "What really matters today?" Make sure your calendar is heavily weighted to take care of your top priorities.

# PART IV. FAITH

## Believe in Something Greater

**B**ECAUSE I PUT faith at the forefront of so much that I do, people who know me or follow my work might expect the FAITH pillar to be the foundation for redefining wealth. However, I intentionally put it after FIT, PEOPLE, and SPACE because I've seen too many people use faith as an excuse not to do the work. As America's Money Maven, I've spoken in dozens of churches, and I talked to many people who wanted a quick fix from God for their finances. They wanted to pray away diabetes or pray their marriage back to health. They said, "Faith without works is dead," but they didn't live like they believed it.

To have the life you want, you have to give God something to bless. If you want your business to grow, you have to launch your product. If you want a promotion, you have to get the certificate required to do the next job. If you want to live a long and healthy life, you have to put in the work to make healthy meals and make time to move daily. It doesn't matter if you're a Christian, a Muslim, or a Jew. It doesn't matter if you're Hindu or Buddhist or your faith practice is an appreciation for the natural world. All the faith in the world can't do the work for you.

While I identify as a follower of the teachings of Jesus Christ, faith, as I talk about it here, isn't a particular religion. This isn't a call for anyone to convert or even to practice Christianity the way I do. I can't tell you what to believe. I can only tell you there's great value in believing in something greater than you or me. Your faith—whatever it may be—is essential to a wealthy life. Understanding and living your faith will prepare you for the valleys you'll inevitably go through as your chase your purpose and it will make the mountaintops that much more fulfilling.

**CHAPTER 10**

# The Power of Faith

THE MESSAGE IN my DMs opened with a bang: "I'm so disappointed in you. I thought you were a real Christian." A woman who followed me on social media had taken time out of her day to chastise me for not being enough of a believer because she hadn't liked the way I handled a recent podcast episode. When I interviewed Brittney Castro, founder of Financially Wise Women, she shared her testimony about being diagnosed with a brain tumor in her early thirties. Brittney talked about how her spiritual teacher helped her get through that difficult period in her life. The woman who messaged me wanted me to know I'd missed my opportunity to tell Brittney that Jesus is our healer and bring her to the Lord.

My perspective was this: at the end of the day, Brittney was alive and well and had gotten through a crisis by leaning on something greater. I would never have interrupted her as she shared her truth to tell her she needed the blood of Jesus. It's not my place to tell people what faith they should practice. I'm unapologetic about my faith, but I won't shun anyone because their beliefs are different from mine. I speak from a Christian perspective and let the way I live my life be my testimony. I don't hide my faith, but I won't condemn anyone for their faith either—just as I wouldn't expect anyone to condemn me for mine.

I've witnessed people struggling with life's blows because they only had a vague idea of what they believed in. The recovery group I participated in a few years ago was a faith-based group, however, two of the women didn't have a faith practice. They wanted to participate, but said they would replace the word "God" with "light" or "love" in our discussions. As she introduced herself, one woman explained, "I don't believe there's some magic person in the sky who has control over everything I'm doing. I believe in free will." She preferred to rely on her own strength and power.

We welcomed those women into our group and allowed them to manage the process their way. However, as the weeks went on and some marriages began to heal, their situations at home seemed to deteriorate. We were all wrestling with our hurt and anger, but they seemed to have an even more difficult time. I can't say I was surprised to watch one and then the other drop out of the twelve-week program. They had nothing to lean on or put their hope in. They had no one greater to whom they could cry out. I firmly believe they would've had an easier time if they'd had a clear faith practice of some kind to which they could turn in the darkest moments. Faith is the secret sauce behind resilience.

## 60. DEFINE YOUR FAITH FOR YOURSELF

So many people have sent me messages to tell me they're not Christian but the podcast has changed their lives in a long list of positive ways. One young woman, who shared with me that she doesn't believe in God, is a faithful listener and sometimes tags me on posts with her progress updates. She wrote to tell me the podcast inspired her to give up smoking cigarettes and stop using recreational drugs. I've never mentioned either of those things, but it's pretty clear they wouldn't fit my definition of a wealthy life. She was inspired, by hearing my podcast guests and my talking about the FIT pillar, to let go of unhealthy habits.

From all appearances, this woman, who I'll call Jane, and I are from completely different walks of life. Not only do we differ in our opinion about God, but we're also from different generations. She's about ten years younger than I am. I'm Black and she's Caucasian. I've never smoked, a habit she's trying to break. Jane has multiple tattoos and piercings on her face, and that's not my thing. Her style is edgy and mine is more traditional. She doesn't fit the demographic of a typical *Redefining Wealth* listener, and she doesn't profess any faith. However, not long ago, during the COVID-19 pandemic lockdown, she posted that she'd found a copy of the "ancient sacred text" I so often talk about in a thrift store and would spend some of her unexpected free time reading it.

When Jane wrote to me or tagged me in her posts, I never pushed her to buy a Bible or look for a church. I never made her wrong for not believing what I believe. I don't know what she'll get from reading the Bible or if she'll ever develop a faith practice anything like mine. I don't know if she'll ever have a relationship with God, but that's not my business. She's clearly challenging herself to grow, and I'm glad to have played a small part in her evolution. *Redefining Wealth* transcends age, ethnicity, gender, orientation, and even religion, but faith is and will always be one of the Six Pillars of Wealth because life is going to happen. Regardless of your chosen belief system, anyone can find value in faith if you have clarity about what you believe. I hope Jane's journey will lead her to her own understanding of faith.

Unlike Jane, I was raised in the church. I sang in the children's choir, memorized and recited verses, participated in Christmas pageants, went to Sunday School, and read the announcements. These were the faith practices my grandmother handed down to me, but I always felt like I was missing something. In church, I'd watch people get the Holy Ghost and wonder why I never felt the same way. "Just keep living," my granny told me when I asked her if something was wrong with them. Over and over, I heard people say through tears, "When I look back over my life and think about the goodness of God!" But I had no idea what they meant.

Fast forward to that fateful moment on the bathroom floor of our tiny apartment in Louisiana. By then, I'd lost a child, lost a home, lost a business and laid off team members I loved. I had spent ten weeks on bed rest, given up our cars, and fled across the country in search of any chance to get our family out of the financial mire we found ourselves in. On that bathroom floor, I couldn't borrow my grandmother's faith. I had to dig down and find my own. I had to decide what I believed in, if I believed what the Bible said, and if I believed what God said about me.

Yes, I still had my work ethic and my knowledge, but neither of those would do me any good without hope, and I found hope in my faith. I found hope in the words, "Of what use is money in the hands of a fool?" at a moment when the money I once had in my hands was all gone. During that trial, which lasted for the next few years, my faith became more defined. What I believed rose to the surface as life tested my faith. When you're in the midst of any kind of crisis and you're mentally spiraling, you may need to stop and define what you believe in. If you believe in anything of substance, you won't be easily pushed over the edge.

It's much easier, of course, to start this search for what you believe while you're in a good place, before you need something to rely on to keep you from falling apart. If you have a "check the right boxes" practice of faith, then get clearer about the tenets of your faith as they apply to your life. If your notion of faith is vague or you have no faith practice at all, but you want one, make a conscious effort to understand different religions and spiritual paths. Check out churches. Talk to people. Don't wait until you're in a global pandemic, deep recession, or personal crisis to look for something to give you more hope and strength. If you're already in the middle of a crisis, then do all that, but do it faster.

Challenge yourself to define what faith means to you and start to practice what you say you believe. Your faith doesn't have to be a religion, but you'd better find something you believe in because life is coming. Some of the best Christians I know, based on the way they live in a Christ-like manner, don't call themselves Christians or profess to believe in God. Those people have a system of values and beliefs that serve as their guiding principles for life. For them, at least at this point, that's enough. I can't tell you how to define your faith, but I can tell you it's incredibly hard to have a wealthy life until you do.

*Redefine Wealth for Yourself*
Clearly articulate what you believe in and where you place your faith. If you're not sure, dedicate some time to exploring different religions, denominations, and spiritual paths until you find a faith practice you can rely on.

# 61. STAND ON SOMETHING OR FALL FOR EVERYTHING

The therapist looked from me to Gerald and back at me again. "If you guys do the work and commit to this process," he told us, "twenty-four months from now, you'll love each other more than ever." I stared back at him and tried not to roll my eyes. In the moment, I wasn't sure I believed the words coming out of his mouth. After all, the mere passage of time pulls a lot of couples apart. We were dealing with something much more serious than growing bored with each other.

After my husband's infidelity, the woman involved launched a nasty campaign of harassment against me. She called and texted me, but social media was her favorite weapon. She used multiple profiles to come after me. If I hadn't had my faith to stand on, I would've fallen for everything she tried to do. I would've let her bad behavior fuel my anger and my hurt. I would've lashed back at her. I would've let resentment grow where I needed forgiveness and mercy to flourish. In all likelihood, I would've given up on my marriage. But because I had my faith to turn to in that dark hour, I didn't give in and engage in a social media war with her or walk away from my marriage. Instead, along with my husband, I did the work. Today, he and I are better friends and lovers than we've ever been.

People often say if you don't stand for something, you'll fall for everything. While there's truth in that, I've also found if you don't stand *on* something, you will fall for anything. Because I stand on the promises of the faith I subscribe to, I recognize that things happen for me, not to me. I know I should be anxious for nothing because what's mine is already mine. God has a plan to prosper me and not harm me, and so as life throws blows I'm not shaken by every little thing.

No matter the situation, I can always stand on my faith. The specific promises I stand on depend on where I need support in my life at a given time. In 2020, my theme for the year was obedience. To grow in this area, one of the verses I turned to often was Deuteronomy 28:2, which promises God's blessings will overtake me if I heed his voice and obey his commandments. All I have to do is keep showing up and doing my part by obeying God's word and God's voice. I stand on that promise.

Once you've defined your faith, it may seem like a vast philosophy almost too big for you to comprehend in a practical way. If so, get down to the micro level. Look at the specific teachings you need to stand on to support you in your life. Expect this list to evolve as the circumstances of your life change. Be clear about what your faith teaches that you can stand on every day as well as when life tries to knock you down.

### Redefine Wealth for Yourself

What can you stand on when life's obstacles rise up? Get clear about the specific promises, laws, or tenets of your faith that will strengthen you and make you more resilient.

## 62. PRACTICE BELIEVING

I was my husband's plus-one for a dinner with one of the most successful reality television producers in the industry, Mark Burnett, and his wife, actor, producer, and author Roma Downey. At the time, Mark Burnett was producing *Funderdome*, a reality competition show featuring entrepreneurs who pitched ideas to win money to fund their startups. When the topic came up over dinner, I naturally shared my thoughts. We had what I thought was a pleasant conversation and ended the night.

The next day, Mark emailed Gerald to offer me an opportunity to serve as a consultant on the show because they were having trouble finding Black contestants. The casting agents were using conventional methods to cast contestants, and they weren't producing the desired results. I happily took the opportunity and ran with it. I reached out to my community and posted on social media. Response from my friends and followers poured in, and the problem was solved.

I didn't go to dinner looking for a job opportunity, but I ended up with a credit as a consulting producer and a check for a consulting fee. I showed up at peace, as who I am, and living in my purpose. I wasn't chasing money, but I attracted it. Behind those kinds of moments in my life is the belief that your gifts will make room for you, one of the many promises the Bible makes. No, I didn't expect my gift for talking to create that particular opportunity, but I firmly believe God has opportunities waiting for me when I operate in my gift.

Your mind is always searching for ways to confirm and affirm your thoughts. As you practice a thought more and more, you solidify it as a belief. If you don't like the results you've created in your life, check your beliefs. Go back to your spiritual text or the framework for your belief system. Understand what it says about you and whatever challenge you're facing. You can believe, based on your own thoughts and observations, that life is hard, or you're not good enough, or people don't want to support you, but what does your belief system say? Practice your faith by believing what your faith says is true.

### Redefine Wealth for Yourself

Practice believing. Choose a belief from your spiritual text or the framework for your faith and go back to it every day. Meditate on it, pray on it, journal about it, and say it out loud until the belief of your faith becomes your personal belief.

## 63. DON'T BE SELECTIVE WITH SURRENDER

I happened to be up at four o'clock in the morning, taking advantage of the quiet time to get work done, when the email landed in my inbox. It was an unexpected invitation to appear on *The Round*, a program in the style of TED Talks, which featured Black women. One of the speakers had dropped out of the upcoming episode, and the producers, who had come across my work online, thought I'd make a great replacement. I was honored to be in a line-up with activists, CEOs, authors and executives from a variety of industries, including Lisa Price, founder of Carol's Daughter, and CEO of the 2008 and 2016 Democratic National Conventions, Leah Daughtry.

Each speaker was expected to come up with a theme for her talk and I chose "listen." Over the next three days, I spent hours writing my presentation, only to have it rejected. Someone else had already chosen that theme, so back to the drawing board I went. With only days left before the show, I sat at my desk wondering what I wanted to share with the audience. Finally, the word "surrender" came to me. It felt right. I created my presentation, the producers approved it, and I flew to New York to give my talk.

After the show aired, dozens of women sent me messages of thanks and shared how they'd been suffering in silence for so long because they hadn't yet learned to surrender. I appreciated the feedback, and in the end, I was glad I'd been forced to rework my talk and had landed on surrender as my theme. I was grateful it helped people, but as I thought more about surrender in the following weeks, I realized I was falling short. There were whole areas in my life in which I wasn't surrendering unto God my goals, my struggles, or my desires.

I'd learned to surrender in my finances because I lost all my money. I'd learned to surrender failure because my business failed. I knew how to surrender very specific things to God, especially when I felt like I had no other choice. However, in other areas, I hadn't yet figured out how to let go. In some aspects of my parenting, in my marriage, in my struggle with secondary infertility, I was still holding on to my ideas of the way things should be. I was trying to force things to go my way.

To surrender is to yield to someone else's power, possession, or control. It doesn't mean giving up on having the life you want. It means surrendering to your Creator or the higher power you believe in so you no longer try to force or manipulate an outcome. It means trusting the process because you understand there's a bigger purpose at work. When you surrender you put your hope in something bigger than you. You take the pressure off yourself to carry a weight beyond your human ability.

Because surrender doesn't always come naturally to me, I'm intentional about it. In my prayer closet, I have a note to myself that reads:

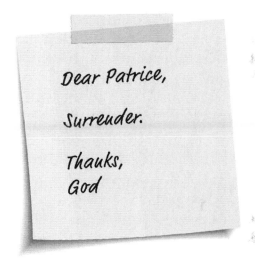

Dear Patrice,

Surrender.

Thanks,
God

Don't be selective with your surrender. Be intentional and allow God to work in every area of your life. Practice your faith by trusting God to deal with people or circumstances beyond your control.

### Redefine Wealth for Yourself

Is surrender a part of your faith? If so, honestly assess where you can improve in this area. Look at each of the Six Pillars of Wealth—FIT, PEOPLE, SPACE, FAITH, WORK, and MONEY— and identify where you need to loosen your grip and surrender those things you can't control anyway.

## 64. WALK IN EXPECTANCY

In 2017, my daughter and I attended the Miss Universe pageant in Las Vegas, and we had a fantastic time. We sat behind some guys who were super fans. They knew all the contestants and lots of stats about them and attended the pageant every year. Their energy was contagious, and I screamed my head off for my favorite contestants. While Miss South Africa took home the crown, Miss Jamaica, Davina Bennett, was my personal favorite. Meeting her in person, I was immediately struck by her presence. She had more than her share of the "it" factor. She was poised and humble and gracious, even when she placed as the second runner-up.

The following Monday, Davina posted on Instagram: "I did not win but I got what I was seeking. I won the hearts of many, I got to highlight Deaf awareness, I stand as the first afro queen to have made it thus far, I represented my little island and I received allll the love one could possibly wish for.... THANK YOU!!! I came, I conquered and if you know me, then you know that's just another story and you will be seeing a lot more from me. To all the queens that represented, congrats and to our new Miss Universe go conquer the world you are indeed a gem!"[8]

Besides gratitude and grace, I read in her post a sense of expectancy. This impressive milestone would be one of many. While she appreciated the experience, Davina made it clear she looked forward to so much more. Her expectancy resonated with me because a similar mindset played such a big part in how I overcame my financial loss. When I was sleeping on my brother's couch and scraping up change to buy diapers, I never once believed I had reached my final destination. I chose to expect God had more in store for me and to act on that belief.

While I chose to walk in expectancy, I tried not to have expectations. An expectation is a strong belief that something specific will happen in the future. As a kid, I expected to go to college, graduate on time, start my business, and ride off into the sunset and live richly ever after. I did the first three, but the last expectation on my list didn't quite work out the way I'd planned. I had expectations of my marriage and of what motherhood would be like, but many of those didn't play out in reality either. I had a beautiful vision of pregnancy and motherhood, but I didn't expect to lose a son before I had my daughter. I didn't expect to fall down the stairs while I was pregnant with her or to spend ten weeks on bed rest. My expectations didn't include my newborn baby spending twenty-one days in the NICU or me leaving the hospital with almost $400,000 in medical debt.

What you look forward to is not always what you get. When you become too attached to your expectations for how everything will be along the way, you lose sight of the bigger vision. Often, expectations are unrealistic because they're based on nothing more than your desires or what you think you know about something you've never experienced. Those expectations can pull your energy and effort in the wrong direction. We all have expectations, but sometimes you're better served by tempering your expectations to make sure they fit the bigger picture of what you want for your life.

Walking in expectancy, on the other hand, means trusting that no matter what happens, all things are working together for your good. Despite what you see, despite what your doctor says, despite what your bank account says or what people are saying about you, expectancy is a decision to trust it's all leading to a greater outcome. It's allowing your faith to boost your confidence. It's trusting that God's promises will be a reality for you and you are moving in that direction.

I say "walking in expectancy" because waiting in expectancy isn't enough. God knows what you're waiting on when he sees what you're working on. In my lifetime, I've heard church people talk way too much about how they're waiting on the Lord. Too often, it's a crutch. It's an excuse. You can't walk into your destiny unless you get up and move. Walk in expectancy, knowing God will bless the work of your hands.

If you want a better marriage, find a counselor. If you want to be a bestselling author, write a great book. If you want to make more money, invest in your personal and professional development. Acknowledge what you don't know and seek wise counsel to fill in those gaps. Then take action and move in the direction of your expectations. While they may not be realized exactly as you envision them, God's promises for you will always be kept.

> ### Redefine Wealth for Yourself
> Are you walking or waiting? Assess your life and your results and determine where you need to not only trust God's promises but take action in the direction of those promises.

## 65. EXPECT RESISTANCE ON THE WAY TO GREATNESS

When Arika Davenport, founder of She Pursues Purpose, told our Purpose 2 Platform group she wanted to host a vision-and-purpose party, the women rallied behind her. Each week, we cheered her on and held her accountable to take action on her goal. However, when the weekend of her event arrived, Arika showed up to the group coaching call on the brink of tears. She shared with the group how everything that could possibly go wrong had gone wrong.

I listened, and after Arika had her say, I reminded her that she was trying to get to the next level of greatness and coming up against resistance was part of the process. "You can't think you're going to skate into this," I told her. We prayed for her, and encouraged her, and Arika moved forward with her plan. She successfully hosted her event, and she has been building her platform and growing her business since then.

I'm not a fan of the saying "new levels, new devils" because it can sound negative, but there's some truth to it, and I'd be remiss if I didn't prepare you for the fact that life is going to happen. It doesn't matter how pumped you are about setting goals and getting results. As you rise in your field or in your next level of accomplishment in any area of life, you will face new challenges. Resistance will surface despite your best efforts, and you'll inevitably have to choose to keep going anyway or give up.

When I researched the concept of resistance for a podcast episode I did on the subject, I came across the concept of electrical resistance, the opposition to current flow in an electrical circuit. All materials offer some level of resistance. With the exception of extreme environmental manipulations, no one has figured out a way to develop a conductor with zero resistance to current flow. In the same way, no human being has figured out how live a life with zero resistance. Certainly, no one has discovered how to achieve greatness without facing resistance along the way.

Expect resistance. Prepare for it and allow it to help you to grow. Have a contingency plan. Think through the obstacles that may occur and prepare for how you'll overcome them. This isn't the same as expecting the worst to happen. You can still expect the best, but when you've thought through potential obstacles, you won't fall apart every time you meet a little—or a lot—of resistance. Even if you don't prepare for a particular circumstance, you'll be prepared to overcome resistance. You'll have faith that there's always a way.

### Redefine Wealth for Yourself

Where are you facing resistance in your life? Where can you expect it to show up? Take the first step to overcome it by praying about the resistance you're facing. Ask for help where you need it and create a plan to overcome it.

## 66. OWN RESILIENCE AS YOUR BIRTHRIGHT

In this book, I've shared so many of the setbacks I've experienced in my life. As a child I experienced the traumas of emotional abuse and seeing a body lying on the street after a drive-by shooting. I've lost a child, lost my businesses, and lost a home. I've dealt with secondary infertility, adultery in my marriage, and the end of friendships I thought would last a lifetime. Still, I get up every day and keep going, and I'm able to do it because I've developed resilience.

According to the American Psychological Association, resilience is "the process of adapting well in the face of adversity, trauma, tragedy, threats, or significant sources of stress—such as family and relationship problems, serious health problems or workplace and financial stressors."[9] Fortunately, resilience isn't a trait you either do or don't have. Even if it takes time for you to develop it, resilience is your birthright. Resilience is the sum total of beneficial behaviors, thoughts, and actions that can be learned and developed in anyone. It's a mindset you can choose.

When I spoke to celebrity life coach Tim Storey on the *Redefining Wealth* podcast, one of his tips to own resilience as your birthright was to remember that being in a drama doesn't mean you have to be dramatic. If you're experiencing a problem or a crisis, you can work it out with dignity. Tim pointed out being dramatic can be as overt as cursing someone out, or it can be as subtle as shifting into victim mode. None of that serves you.

Just as crises are an inevitable part of life, so is change. Certain goals you once had may no longer be attainable in the way you thought they would be. Accept that circumstances have changed and keep realistic goals in front of you. Small accomplishments can still move you toward the results you want. Instead of focusing on tasks that seem unachievable, ask yourself, "What's one thing I can accomplish today to move me in the direction I want to go?"

Finally, look for opportunities for self-discovery. If you take the time to reflect, you can always learn something about yourself from the way you handle setbacks. Use that information to grow. Many people who have experienced tragedies and hardship report improved relationships, greater strength, an increased sense of self-worth, a more developed spiritual life, and a heightened appreciation for life. Choose resilience and allow life's hardships to serve you rather than take you down.

### Redefine Wealth for Yourself

Look back on the ways you've handled setbacks in the past. What are the greatest losses you've suffered? How did they change you? What lessons can you learn from them? How can those lessons help you grow stronger and more resilient?

## CHAPTER 11

# Practice What You Say You Believe

ONE WEEKEND IN the fall of 2019, I locked myself in a hotel room to work on this book. Prior to that, I'd traveled to twelve cities in seven weeks. I'd been so busy coaching, speaking, and recording that checking into a hotel was the only way I could shut out the distractions and make time to write. Sitting alone in my hotel room with nowhere to race off to, I realized my book wasn't the only thing I'd neglected during in recent months. I'd also neglected my FAITH pillar. It had a slot on my calendar, but I was going through the motions, doing the quick and easy stuff.

I'd reached a point when I wanted to know God for myself. Rather than depend on what a preacher said, I wanted to study the history and the text and ask questions to find my own answers. However, instead of going down deep into the Word, I was snacking on devotionals here, a scripture there, some praise music here, a prayer there. My faith snacking habit left me spiritually malnourished, and I saw the symptoms in my life.

Unless you consume the right nutrients in adequate amounts, eating regularly won't leave you well nourished. You can snack on empty calories all day, and while you may feel full, your body will tell a different story as, over time, your bones become brittle and your muscles weaken. You become sluggish and prone to illness and infection. Your eyesight deteriorates. Minor cuts and wounds take longer than usual to heal, and you suffer constipation. Physical malnutrition causes a failure to thrive.

In the same way, spiritual malnutrition prevents you from growing and flourishing in your faith. In my case, my patience became brittle, my mental endurance weakened, and I struggled to carry the kind of heavy load I once managed with ease. I lacked the energy and enthusiasm I like to bring to everything I do. I was susceptible to negative thoughts infecting my mind, and I had a hard time letting things go and allowing emotional wounds to heal. My spirit was begging for sustenance.

When you're spiritually nourished, on the other hand, you don't take other people's words and behaviors personally. Because you know who you are, you're not susceptible to what anyone says about you. Because you're constantly renewing your mind, no one can plant seeds of doubt or regret to keep you from moving forward in your life. You can be patient with other people's imperfections, and you have more energy, enthusiasm, and stamina to go after what you want.

When you give your spirit the rich nourishment required to thrive, you become strong enough to let go of suffering and stop nursing old wounds. You have the capacity to heal quickly and move on. Dreams and goals that were once stuck and stagnating can finally flow and move. You become strong enough to accept and sustain the abundance and the enlarged territory you've been praying to receive.

Alone in that hotel room, I decided it was time for me to stop living on spiritual trail mix and sit down for balanced meals. I started by making time to study the Bible, my spiritual text, with a goal of developing a richer understanding of the context and the key players. In the following weeks and months, my symptoms of spiritual malnutrition lessened, and I felt much better equipped to handle both the obstacles and the opportunities that came up in my life every day.

When you're starving for more spiritual sustenance, it's tempting to try fill that emptiness with other things, but it never works. Spiritual malnutrition hinders your spiritual growth. It also keeps you stuck in other areas of your life, including your ability to produce, maintain, and sustain wealth. If you feel like, no matter what you try, you can't seem to get any momentum in your health, your relationships, your space, your work, or your money, examine how you're sustaining your spirit. Practice what you say you believe by going beyond the surface of your faith. Let the act of regularly nourishing your spirit support you in every area of your life.

## 67. MAKE TIME, DON'T FIND TIME

At the beginning of a new year, a young woman in my free Facebook community asked a question about the WORK pillar. While she believed she'd done all the right things, she lived in Trinidad and Tobago, where money was tight, and she wasn't seeing progress with her business. As our conversation continued, I got the feeling her struggle didn't have anything to do with work, and I suggested she take a step back from focusing on her WORK pillar.

She was clearly smart and willing to put in the work. However, her tone and some of her word choices—using phrases like "nobody on my island" and other absolutes—led me to believe she hadn't paid enough attention to her FAITH pillar. She wasn't walking in expectancy. Every day, she spent hours and hours going in circles, trying to force results in her WORK pillar, but she didn't give her FAITH pillar nearly as much attention because she didn't make time.

You don't get what you want; you get what you believe. I suggested she change her language and the way she talked about her opportunities to develop her belief in what was possible for her. Her language was bleak and pessimistic and affected the way she showed up for every sales conversation, every proposal, and every meeting. Of course, potential clients told her no when she wanted to hear yes. She had decided in advance that would be the case. She believed nothing was available to her, so nothing was available to her.

Since she was also dealing with health conditions, I suggested she go all in on her fitness and her faith for a while. A couple of weeks later, she came back and shared her testimony. She was eating better, reading a Proverb each day, and praying more. With those changes, she was inspired to clean and organize her room. She listened to a few episodes of the *Redefining Wealth* podcast and decided to let go of her pessimistic attitude. Her whole attitude around her ability to have a profitable business improved.

Many people think they're too busy to practice what they say they believe. They can't find time to work on their FAITH pillar, but you don't find time for what matters. You make time, which refers to the SPACE pillar. If faith matters to you, put it on your calendar, like you would an important meeting or a doctor's appointment.

It's easy to relegate faith to Sunday morning, but if you want to enjoy the full benefits of your faith and its promises to you, faith has to be a substantial part of your daily life. If you ate, showered, or brushed your teeth only once a week, you'd have a problem. If I only called my mama once a week, she'd threaten to divorce me. Once a week isn't enough for something you say is a priority. Anything you want to improve in life requires an investment of time, and practicing your faith is no different.

### Redefine Wealth for Yourself

Are you giving your faith the time it deserves in your schedule? If your faith practices are hit or miss, open your calendar now. Choose a consistent time to pray, study, or meditate on the sacred text of your faith each day. Block that time on your calendar, and guard it as you would your most important appointment.

## 68. GET UP WHEN YOU WAKE UP

When I was twenty-five years old, pregnant with my son, and on bed rest, I had the same dream over and over. A few times each week, I woke up at three o'clock in the morning after dreaming I was with Gerald and a little girl. In the dream, people kept saying to us, "She looks just like her dad." When I told Gerald about the dream, he and I joked about how off-base it was because we were having a little boy.

Nothing in my life would have made me think I was going to lose my son. I was on bed rest, but I was young and healthy. My business brought in plenty of money, and my life was going well. I had no reason to expect tragedy, even though it waited for me right around the corner. In hindsight, I can see that God used my recurring dream to prepare me for the fact that my son was going to pass. At the same time, he offered me comfort by showing me Reagan, the little girl I would have and raise. I was able to receive God's message in the middle of the night, when all was quiet around me, and because I woke up each time I had the dream, I remembered exactly what God had shown me.

I didn't realize what the dream meant until after I lost my son, and even if I had, I couldn't have changed those events. All I could do was hold on to the image of that beautiful little girl. However, there are times when God wakes you up in the middle of the night because you need to take action before it's too late. Earlier, I shared the story of a team member who attempted to sabotage my business after I let her go. When I woke up at three in the morning and heard God tell me to check an account or change a password, there turned out to be a very good reason. Had I not decided to be obedient and get up and do what I was told, she could have done much more serious damage to my business.

One of my mentors, George Thompson, talked about this principle—get up when you wake up—as a productivity tip. He suggested if you happened to wake up in the early morning hours, you should take advantage of the time by getting up and starting your day. That can be good advice when you have a lot to do. However, I've also found the stillness of those early morning hours makes it much easier for me to listen and hear from the Holy Spirit. When I wake up at these unexpected times in the middle of the night, it gives God a chance to speak to me without interruption.

Sometimes, when you wake up after midnight, it's not a bathroom break. The Holy Spirit may be trying to get your attention, and the only way to know is to stop and listen. You may hear that it's time to take action on something. If so, don't put it off. Get up when you wake up and be obedient. If you say you believe God speaks to you, then do what God tells you to do—even if you have to get out of the bed to do it.

> **Redefine Wealth for Yourself**
> When you wake up in the middle of the night, don't lie there frustrated and worrying about how tired you'll be the next afternoon. Listen. What's God telling you? When you receive instruction, get up and take action right away.

## 69. SET UP A SACRED SPACE

In 2019, Carla Williams, a member of Mastery + Momentum, started to crave more quiet in her life. The blogger, wife, and mother of two small girls wanted to start her days by spending more time with God, so she finally settled on waking up at 5:30 every morning. That way, she had a solid hour to devote to her FAITH pillar before her family required her attention. Carla played worship songs to set the tone in her sacred space. She worked through devotionals, read the Bible, wrote in her journal, and prayed. At the end of each hour, she spent some time in silence, listening to whatever the Lord wanted to say to her.

That summer, Carla was under significant stress from her job search. Her husband was sending out her resume for her, but she wasn't sure she wanted a corporate job. One day, while she was in her sacred space, spending time with God, the Lord revealed he had a plan for Carla and told her to stop applying for jobs. Carla told her husband not to submit her resume anywhere else. She was trusting God and allowing His plan for her to reveal itself.

A few months later, Carla heard from a friend she hadn't talked to in several years. This friend was searching for a candidate to fill a position. The job description for the leadership role wasn't a perfect match for Carla's resume, but she was qualified and it would be a significant step up from her last position. Her friend encouraged her to apply.

Carla sailed through the hiring process with confidence because, during her time in her sacred space, God had confirmed the job was for her. One month later, Carla was offered a job as vice president of marketing. If she hadn't made time to listen to God, if she hadn't created a sacred space in her life to practice her faith, she might have missed that opportunity. Instead, she would almost certainly have been offered and have taken another job, one that wouldn't have advanced her career in the way her position as a vice president did.

Carla didn't have a spare room or a walk-in closet to use as her sacred space. With two small children, the only place she could be alone to communicate with God and not wake up the girls, was a bathroom. It wasn't her dream prayer closet, but she made it work, and the new job was just one of the benefits Carla got from that dedicated time with God. She became more patient and found herself reaching out more, extending herself to others, offering to pray for friends, receiving revelations for them, and sharing those revelations.

In my prayer room, I keep the things that support me—my prayer journal, pictures of people I'm praying for, images of things I'm believing for, candles, and faith-based books. Now that I have a dedicated sacred space, I leave those things on display, but once upon a time, I too used a bathroom as my sacred space. Sometimes, you have to grab a bathroom, a closet, or the corner of a bedroom and work with what you have available.

If your sacred space also serves other purposes, prayer coach Jazlyn Denise suggests you fill a box with items to support you in your practice and bring them in and out as needed. Lighting a single candle or hanging a picture can be enough, and don't worry if the room is small. The size of the space doesn't make it sacred. The sacred nature comes from how you treat the space and the intention you bring to your time there.

### Redefine Wealth for Yourself

Look around your home and identify a corner, closet, or room to utilize as your sacred space. Add something, like a candle, a journal, or a symbol of your faith, to remind you of the new purpose the space will serve. Dedicate a time of day to study, pray, or otherwise nurture your faith there.

## 70. FIND A PRAYER PARTNER

I believe the Bible when it says when two or more believers gather in God's name, God is in our midst. That's why, for more than a decade, I've had prayer partners. At this point in my life, I have different prayer partners for different areas of my life. We may focus on family, business, health, or other areas where we seek God's blessings. One partnership consists of three women, including me. When we meet, I pray over the first woman, who prays over the second, who prays over me. This set-up works for us, but there's no limit to how you can create your prayer partnership.

Prayer partners have been a secret weapon in my spiritual warfare because, sometimes, you have to borrow someone else's faith when you're in the midst of a trial. You don't always have the words or strength to pray for yourself when you need it most. That's when your prayer partner can step in for you and pray on your behalf. In a reciprocal relationship, that prayer goes both ways, and you can speak life over someone else in a way you might hesitate to do for yourself. When you hear those words in your own voice, spoken for someone else's benefit, it's a reminder of what's possible for you.

Your prayer partner can give you a nudge when you suffer from spiritual amnesia. Once you pray and turn a problem or a desire over to God, it's easy to forget what you asked God to do for you. At times, you might not recognize the answer to your prayer when you receive it because you've forgotten you asked for it. However, a good prayer partner will remind you how you prayed together for that very thing. Of course, you can serve your prayer partner in the same way.

A relationship with a prayer partner holds you accountable to practice what you say you believe. It multiplies the strength of your prayers for your benefit and for theirs. It gives you a place to share praise reports and celebrate what God has done for you. It gives you a place to be vulnerable and share what's really going on in your life. As your relationship with your prayer partner grows and deepens over time, you'll become more comfortable sharing your weaknesses and your struggles. Sharing your test and your testimony with your prayer partner can remove any shame and allow you to recognize you're never alone.

*Redefine Wealth for Yourself*
Pray and think about who in your circle would make a good prayer partner. Invite that person to join you in prayer at a consistent time every week, meeting by phone or video conference. Don't worry if the first partnership doesn't work out. You may have to ask more than one person and try more than one set-up before you discover exactly what works for you. Keep trying until you create a prayer partnership that works for everyone involved and commit to praying together for the next six to twelve months.

## 71. DIVE DEEPER INTO YOUR SACRED TEXT

When I was younger, I thought I wasn't a true Christian, or maybe my faith wasn't strong enough, because I couldn't memorize Bible verses well. I could paraphrase a verse and tell you if it came from the New Testament or the Old Testament, but that was about it. If you wanted me to quote book, chapter, and verse, you were out of luck. As I've matured in my faith, I speak life over my memory and recognizing that, like any other skill, I can improve in this area. However, I've also learned there's more to studying the sacred text of my faith than memorizing Bible verses.

To glean more from my time in the Bible, I started to read more deeply, and now I read for quality rather than quantity. I read for understanding and application. I'm still the queen of paraphrasing Scripture, but what I once thought of as a weakness, has turned into a strength. Putting it in my own words helps me apply the Word to my life.

In the Bible, when Nehemiah returned to Jerusalem to rebuild the walls around the city, he was doing a great and important work. People tried to entice him to stop working on the wall that would protect his city, but Nehemiah refused to come down. Even as I wrote this book, I had people and projects vying for my attention, but I reflected on Nehemiah's story. This book was an important project for me and I wanted it to be a great work. I was writing it to give people a tool to transform their lives.

So no, I would not be tempted to come down from my wall. I wouldn't be distracted. Having that story to turn to and understanding how it applied to my life helped me stay focused.

These days, I read the Bible more slowly. I stop to look up unfamiliar words. I endeavor to understand the historical and cultural context. I want to understand why certain things happened and certain decisions were made. I dive deeper into familiar stories and passages. I take time to analyze them and understand how they might apply to a modern context by retelling the stories in ways that apply to life as I know it.

Study your spiritual text like you would study for an exam in your favorite class in school. Expand your reading to learn about the time and place in which the text was written. Commit passages, stories, and scriptures to memory so that, when a trial arises, you can lean into them and connect the dots to your circumstances. Summarize the words and the stories and make them your own. Immerse yourself in this book you've chosen as your manual for life.

### Redefine Wealth for Yourself

Create a plan for practical study of your faith so you can dive deeper into your sacred text. Buy a book, take a class, or join an existing Bible study or study group, so you have a structure for your plan, and stick to it.

## CHAPTER 12

# Demonstrate Your Faith in Real Life

L UNCH STARTED AS a fun girlfriend get-together. Sitting on a restaurant patio in the Los Angeles sunshine, Jamila (not her real name) and I caught up on each other's lives. The conversation soon turned to her ex-boyfriend, and chuckling, we found him on social media. The fun stopped when Jamila saw he was married with a child. My girlfriend, single and with no children of her own at the time, glared at her smiling ex with his wife and kid and made an incredibly unkind comment about his little girl.

She was speaking from a place of hurt feelings, but Jamila's words shocked me. That wasn't the kind of woman I knew her to be. Besides, she and her ex had broken up years earlier. I thought she had long since moved beyond the pain of his betrayal. Instead, she was prolonging her suffering by reflecting on the relationship from a place of anger and vengefulness. Jamila held herself out as a practicing Muslim, so I asked her, "Friend, what does the Quran say about forgiveness?"

She gave me a side eye and said, "I don't know."

I'm certainly not a Quran scholar, but I'm pretty sure Islam, like Christianity, encourages forgiveness. My friend's unwillingness to yield to the teachings of her faith left me wondering what her faith really meant to her. Of course, I can never know her heart. Maybe she was having a bad day. But what I observed was someone willing to go through all the motions of faith when certain people were watching, but who put her faith aside when its principles became inconvenient for her. To embrace the teachings of her faith, she needed to do the work to forgive her ex, as she would want Allah to forgive her.

I don't want to minimize what Jamila went through. The relationship caused her tremendous pain, but she was choosing to stay stuck in it. No matter how wonderful her life looked on the outside, inside, she was still in turmoil. She had all the trappings of success, but she didn't have peace. If she can lean into her faith and endeavor to demonstrate her faith in real life, I believe she'll quickly find her way out of that dark place.

It's one thing to wear your religion on the outside, but your faith doesn't get real until you demonstrate it in real life even when you'd rather not. Regardless of your faith, religion, denomination, or spiritual beliefs, creating a wealthy life requires you to live what you say you believe. Interestingly, the world's major religions share many common values. Jews, Christians, and Muslims all believe in one God who created the Earth. Buddhism doesn't teach its followers to believe in any god, but the philosophy still shares some tenets with major religions. They all prioritize people over materialism and encourage followers to seek something higher than themselves. They teach that you will reap what you sow and your actions in this life will have consequences in the next.

Whatever your spiritual path, the teachings of your faith are more than words on a page. They're meant to be lived. If you struggle to handle the typical challenges of life, like break-ups, disappointments at work, financial challenges, or differences of opinion with people in your life, consider examining how you can better demonstrate your faith every day. My girlfriend said she was Muslim and went through the motions of religious rituals, but when it came down to it, she wasn't living her faith. Of course, she's not alone. So many people say they're Christians, but even as they wear a cross around their neck, they make choices that directly contradict the teachings of Jesus Christ. When you don't live your life according to the spiritual practice you claim to follow, you do the collective followers of your faith more harm than good because you fail to represent the best of your faith.

## 72. FORGIVE PEOPLE WHO WILL NEVER SAY I'M SORRY

During one of the most difficult times of my life, a woman I considered a mentor, a mama figure, and a friend turned her back on me. This was the woman who taught me much of what I know about how to carry myself as a woman in the world—how to dress, how to talk, how to maintain a comfortable home. A lot of what she showed me I hadn't seen growing up. I marveled, for example, at how she always had pictures hung, walls painted, and well-chosen accessories even when she lived in apartments. She introduced me to a new level of class, and when I bought my first condo, much of my decor was passed on to me from her house.

When she went through a hard time financially and my business was doing well, I gladly helped this friend. When she paid me back, I was grateful, but I was also proud to have been in a position to help her. After my business fell apart with the crash of the housing market, she introduced me to people who gave me work when I needed it. For a time in my life, I saw her almost every day, and when she needed anything, I gladly pitched in. We were incredibly close, and I could never have imagined she would betray me. But she did.

I was being harassed online, my husband and I were doing our best to recover from his infidelity, and rather than support me, this friend shut me out. Mutual friends told me she'd gone on a rant about how dumb I was to stay in my marriage, insisting I must have something seriously wrong with my self-esteem. While she spoke to others about my situation, not once did she pick up the phone to call or text me to see how I was doing. My husband reached out to her and encouraged her, regardless of how she felt about him, to communicate with me, but it never happened.

In therapy, I learned that to forgive is to give up the possibility that the past could have been any different from what it was. When I spoke with Pastor Geremy Dixon of Center of Hope Church, in Inglewood, California, on my podcast, he echoed the sentiment when he said playing an offense over and over in your mind only impacts you. To forgive this woman, I had to stop rehearsing all the ways things could have gone differently or better in our relationship. It doesn't matter what I wish had happened or what I wish she had done. I had to accept the way things were.

I'm willing to forgive because I never want anyone else's behavior to make me become someone I don't want to be. For example, to allow one scenario and my unforgiveness around it to define how I build relationships moving forward would be foolish. I could easily extrapolate her behavior to all women and put up walls, but I went in the other direction. I created Purpose 2 Platform and Mastery + Momentum on the heels of this betrayal. Building communities where women feel safe asking for support from one another and being vulnerable about their lives and their businesses was only possible because I didn't allow one person's behavior to color how I saw every woman.

Forgiveness is a gift you give yourself, not something you do for the other person. Harboring unforgiveness for one person can negatively affect your other relationships by causing you to become mistrustful, cold, or distant. Protect the personal relationships that mean the most to you by developing a habit of forgiveness.

### Redefine Wealth for Yourself

Investigate any offenses for which you're holding a grudge. Ask yourself the following questions as suggested by Pastor Dixon:

1. Do I feel offended not because something was wrong but because I wanted it a different way?
2. Am I ready to give up the possibility that it could have happened differently?

When it makes sense to do so and the relationship is one that, after evaluation, you decide you want to maintain, sit with the offender and have an open dialogue about what happened. Ask questions for clarity and avoid placing blame. Whether or not you receive an apology, make peace with the past and let go of the possibility that it could have gone differently.

## 73. EXTEND GRACE REGULARLY

One day, I was venting to my friend Ashley and complaining about how my husband needed to improve in certain areas of his life. When I paused for a breath, Ashley said, "You got to fix all your junk on your own timeline, but you're trying to put him on your timeline." She pointed out that Gerald doesn't come to me with books he wants me to read or podcasts he wants me to listen to. He doesn't push me to learn the lessons he's learned or change based on his latest priorities. My husband lets me grow at my own pace.

Ashley was right. Having known me for almost two decades, she was well aware of my passion for personal and professional development. I've pursued both at my own pace, but I tried to micromanage Gerald's journey and get him to evolve on my timeline. I wanted to choose the content he consumed, and I wanted him to get the lessons when I did. My desire for us to grow together was well intentioned, but it wasn't fair to him.

In her *Redefining Wealth* podcast interview, Christine Hassler, described letting each person evolve on their own timeline as giving people the dignity of their own process. When I let my husband find his way, slowly but surely, he discovers the process best suited to him. He gets the message he needs to get from the messenger who resonates with him. When I extend that grace, I also take away the judgment and expectations that can strain any relationship.

You want the best for the people you love, but it's not up to you to dictate their process. Instead of trying to fix them, make sure they know you love them unconditionally. Hold a safe space for them to learn and develop without judgment. Demonstrate your faith by trusting God to work it out and get them where they need to be.

### Redefine Wealth for Yourself

The next time you catch yourself trying to nag or nudge someone to grow and develop the way you want, stop. Apologize for your pushiness and express your support instead of your judgment.

## 74. FIGHT FOR GRATITUDE

More than 15,000 women attended the California Women's Conference the year I hosted a panel for the event. After my turn onstage, the women shared so much positive feedback, and I enjoyed talking to them. A few of the women told me they'd enjoyed my panel so much they wished I was a main-stage speaker. It felt encouraging to hear they benefited from my contribution, but as I told them, I was grateful to have been invited to host a panel.

Not everyone, however, enjoyed the event. One woman introduced herself to me as a pastor and motivational speaker and told me she was scheduled to participate in a panel later in the day. I started to congratulate her, but she cut me off to inform me I shouldn't have done the panel. She implied hosting a panel was beneath me, but I assured her it had been my pleasure to do it. This was my first invitation to speak in any capacity at a conference of that magnitude. I'd only recently introduced myself to the world as America's Money Maven, and the event provided me with excellent exposure. Hosting the panel felt like a huge win.

Even after I expressed my perspective, she continued. She picked apart every aspect of the event. As she talked, she looked to me for confirmation, as if she expected me to commiserate with her, but I couldn't. Maybe everything she said was true. Maybe there were issues with the event, but I focused on what had gone right, and I felt grateful.

That speaker and I share the same faith. Our faith teaches us all things work for our good and to count it all joy even when circumstances don't seem to go our way, because God is always working in our favor. If we believe those things, we can find the positive in any situation. At the very least, we should actively search for it.

You can't be an example of faith if you're walking around in victimhood all the time. If you want to demonstrate your faith in real life, fight to find the good in everything you experience. In every situation, find a blessing or a lesson and be grateful for either. When you do, your gratitude will encourage other people. They'll be drawn to you. They'll be curious about the faith that allows you to live this way, and you'll have the satisfaction of knowing you've represented your faith well.

> ### Redefine Wealth for Yourself
> Develop a habit of finding the good in every situation. When you want to complain, check yourself by asking, "Blessing or lesson?" Identify one or the other and express your appreciation for it.

## 75. OPERATE IN INTEGRITY

The first time I received a call to appear as a guest expert on Steve Harvey's nationally syndicated television show, I really wanted to make it happen. The show would allow me to share my message with a large audience, many of whom had never heard of me. On top of that, a sponsor had offered me $15,000 to do the seven-minute segment and share their message along with mine. I said yes to the producer, and a few minutes later, the talking points arrived in my inbox.

As I read through the script, I realized I'd spoken too soon. The sponsor's message conflicted with my own. I couldn't appear on television in front of millions of people and give the masses advice I wouldn't give a close girlfriend. I'd worked too hard to build trust with my audience, and I'd have to be dishonest and out of integrity to say what the sponsor wanted me to say. It had seemed like the opportunity I'd been waiting for, but it turned out not to be. I emailed the producer within minutes and explained why I had to pass.

Two months later, the producer reached out to me again. She respected that I'd stuck to my convictions the first time around, and she had another opportunity for me. Once again, it was a sponsored segment. "This time," the producer explained, "you can adjust the script however you like." I accepted the offer and made the changes necessary changes to the script. I maintained my integrity by delivering content I believed in, and I still drove sales for the sponsor.

That appearance was the beginning of my stint as a regular guest on the talk show.

My faith teaches me to tell the truth, to love my neighbor as myself, and to not be hypocritical. I can't just say I'm a follower of Christ; I have to live by the teachings of Jesus when it's easy to do and when it's difficult. Operating in integrity by living by those principles sometimes requires a sacrifice, but I do it because I want to live my faith. I'm not perfect, but I do my best not to cross the line.

Actions and choices out of alignment with the beliefs you claim to hold undercut your ability to witness for your faith. If you say you're a practitioner of Christianity, Islam, or another faith, live accordingly. When you choose otherwise, you're out of integrity. Your hypocrisy hurts the image of your faith, and it hurts you. Without fail, it will damage your reputation and impede your long-term goals. Be aware of how you model your faith for other people. If you profess to follow a particular faith, live it.

> ### Redefine Wealth for Yourself
> Make a list of the most important tenets of your faith, the standards by which your faith calls you to live. When you make small or significant decisions check in with yourself to make sure you're in alignment with the faith you profess to practice.

## 76. BE THE WALKING CONTRADICTION

The first time I spoke to a wide audience about filing bankruptcy was during an appearance on a national news show. Around the same time, I shared the story in a two-page spread in the *New York Post*. Right there in black and white, under pictures of my family and me, I recounted how I'd built and lost a seven-figure business. I'd already shared those details many times, one on one and from the stage, but I'd never talked about it on a platform where millions of people could read or hear it.

I chose to go big with the story because a few people were threatening to "expose" it. They were under the mistaken impression that I was ashamed and wanted to keep my financial losses a secret. In truth, shame had nothing to do with it, and I'd already told so many people that I never thought of it as a secret. I didn't mind sharing my story because I knew it all happened for me and not to me. Hitting my financial low gave me a new sense of compassion for people struggling with money. It gave me a testimony people could relate to and be inspired by. In the end, it all worked for my good, and I had no problem talking about it.

When you step out to do something new, don't be surprised if haters from your past show up to poke at you. They'll watch everything you do and try to pick it apart, questioning your worth and your legitimacy in an attempt to make you second guess yourself. The haters want to convince you that you don't have the right to stand up, speak out, or be seen. They want you to ask yourself, "Who am I to do something so big?" They want you to fall for their fictional version of your story, a version that always ends with you as the loser. If you allow them to, they haters will shame you into sitting down and shutting up.

Acknowledge the facts of your story and you take away the haters' power. Own those facts, like I owned my bankruptcy, and no one can use them to shame you. At the same time, realize that's just a small part of your story. You can't go back and change the past, but you can learn from it. You can grow, move on, and do better.

No one can tell how your story ends by looking at one moment or event in your life. Instead of allowing them to convince you of a lie, turn to what your faith says about you. Contradict their fiction with God's promises and how those promises are being made manifest in your life. When they expect you to hang your head in shame, hold your head high and walk into the destiny God has for you. Be their walking contradiction.

> **Redefine Wealth for Yourself**
> If you find yourself falling for the lies other people tell, or which
> you tell yourself, about the facts of your life, go back to Chapter 2
> and work through the "What IF vs. What IS" exercise to get clear
> about your truth. Then, take the stories holding you captive and
> put them through a model of fact, fiction, and contradiction.
>
> Here's an example:
> **Fact:** In 2008, I lost all my money, and in 2009, I had to sleep
> on my brother's couch.
>
> **Fiction:** I was destined to never have anything and sleep on
> the couch forever.
>
> **Contradiction:** I lost all my money in 2009, and by 2010 I was
> creating a personal finance consulting empire.

## 77. SHARE THE MIDDLE

On Easter Sunday of 2020, I heard a sermon by Mike Todd of
Transformation Church, in Tulsa, Oklahoma, in which he talked about
how we tell the story of Jesus's resurrection by focusing on Good Friday
and Resurrection Sunday.[10] However, we skip the Saturday. We skip the
middle. The message resonated with me because, when I first started
telling the story of how I lost my son, I tended to skip the middle. I shared
many times the story of how my son died, in 2006, after just five hours in
my arms. However, I often made it sound like my son passed and then,
in no time, I had Reagan because I rarely shared the middle of the story.

When I went into labor with my son, my friend took me to Daniel
Freeman Hospital in Inglewood. I was twenty-five years old, but I looked
about fifteen. Whether because of my apparent youth, my race, or any
combination of factors, the emergency room staff completely dismissed
my pleas for help. They left me doubled over in pain for hours. My friend

and the other people in the waiting room begged them to see me, but the staff refused. At one point, a woman came over and put her hand on my back and prayed for me. A man across from me was bleeding badly, but when they called his name, he asked them to take me instead.

The doctor on duty sent me home with Tylenol, but later that day, my mom had to take me to Cedars-Sinai Hospital. There, my son was born prematurely and passed away, and the doctor informed me I could have died of sepsis had I not come to Cedars when I did. In this country, Black women die of pregnancy-related causes at a rate two to six times higher than white women.[11] I would've been another statistic.

After I lost my son, I returned to Faithful Central Bible Church, where I'd once been a regular attendee. At the end of one mid-week service, a woman asked several people for a ride. I lived five minutes from the church, but I offered to take her home. As we finally neared her destination, she said, "God wants me to tell you to remember he's faithful. His compassion will fail you not. His mercy is new every morning." Then, she said, "You're going to have another baby."

I hadn't told her about losing my son. I hadn't even mentioned it in church, so I asked her, "Have I met you before?" When she said no, I explained that I'd lost my son eight weeks earlier. I told her the story of how I'd gone to the first hospital, but no one had helped me.

Now it was her turn to look surprised. "Are you the young lady I prayed for?" she asked. "You were doubled over in pain, so I never saw you face, but God told me to pray for you."

As we pulled up to her destination, she told me to read Lamentations, and then, she was gone. I didn't see which way she went, and I never saw her again, but I followed her suggestion. When I got to Lamentations 3:22-23, I read, "It is because of the Lord's mercy *and* loving-kindness that we are not consumed, because His [tender] compassions fail not. They are new every morning; great *and* abundant is Your stability and faithfulness."

Those were also the words from a song I'd listened to over and over in the weeks since I lost my son. I sang along every day, but I had no clue the words were taken from Scripture. That day, I decided to stop listening to the enemy telling me I'd lost my son because I was being punished for getting pregnant out of wedlock or something else I'd done wrong. The message that woman delivered from God changed the way I viewed my situation and handled my grief. Inspired by my conversation with her, I made it to deliverance. I made it to my Resurrection Sunday because I chose to believe what God said about me. That was the middle of my story.

By not sharing the middle for so many years, I'd cheated the people who needed to know getting through was possible for them too. So often we skip the middle when we tell our story because that's the hard part. It reveals who you are, and you can't always tell it in a quick sound-bite. Instead we say, "I was broke, and now I'm rich. I was sick, and now I'm healed." We tell these stories every day, but we don't tell what happened between the beginning and the end.

In Command the Stage, my program for transformational speak-ers, and in Purpose 2 Platform, I've encountered women with powerful stories they couldn't bring themselves to share. They were embarrassed or afraid of what people would think. They worried about being judged, but whether they know your story or not, people are always judging you. When you tell your story, you help anyone who's listening build their faith. Hearing what you've been through, overcome, and achieved helps people believe in what's possible for them. When you see your stories as your personal ministry, you don't hide them or hoard them. You own them, you shape them, and you share them to serve others.

When you share the middle of your story, you demonstrate your faith. God is served when you let people see those interim steps and recognize how your faith carried you through. It doesn't matter if your platform is five people, five million, or the one person who needs to talk to you. You have an opportunity to be an example of your faith by sharing the whole story.

### Redefine Wealth for Yourself

Write out a story of when your faith helped you overcome. Pay attention to the middle. Describe what you went through, who showed up for you, and how God worked in your life so you could come out victorious on the other side. The next time you tell someone your story, tell the middle too.

# PART V. WORK

## Live Your Life's Purpose

WHEN I CAME up with the tagline, "Chase purpose, not money," a few years ago, I'd already lived this way for a long time. Since I started my first business, I've used my gifts to do purposeful work in some way. Over time, I've refined and clarified what that looks like, and my purpose has evolved. God has given you the same ability to produce material wealth with your talents, gifts, and experiences while pursing your purpose. Doing so glorifies him, serves other people, and helps you find fulfillment. This is why the WORK pillar focuses not just on finding the right job but on living your life's purpose.

When you're fired up to work in your purpose, it has a positive impact on all the other pillars. You no longer have a need to shop, eat, or drink to fill a void in your life, and you can easily define your priorities. When you're working for more than a paycheck, you bring a spirit of enthusiasm to everything you do. You naturally strive to operate in excellence, and you attract people and opportunities that would have otherwise passed you by. You can live every day knowing you're answering the calling on your life.

## CHAPTER 13

# Accept Your Purpose

ONE DAY, I recorded an entire webinar, ninety-five minutes of my best material, and the recording didn't download. I lost every bit of it, and I was on the verge of freaking out because I'd put so much time and effort into it. When Reagan came into the room and found out what happened, she was calm and reassuring. "Mom," she said, "I bet it'll be so much better than the first time when you do it again." She was in third grade, and with no prompting or guidance, she knew exactly what to say to comfort me. This is one of her gifts.

Reagan can listen to anybody talk about anything and show genuine empathy. She makes people feel like she's really listening to them, and she is. Her school friends seek her advice when they have problems at home or at school because they trust that she cares. Reagan didn't have to work to develop her compassionate nature. It was given to her freely. It's a gift, and I believe this and her other gifts will make it possible for her to fulfill her purpose in life—as long as she accepts her purpose. If, like so many people, she makes the mistake of choosing instead to chase a dream based on a passion but out of alignment with her gifts and her purpose, she'll struggle to find fulfillment or create success for herself.

People use the terms gift, passion, and purpose in different ways, so I want to be very clear about how I use each of these words.

**Gifts:** the skills and abilities that come naturally to you. You may have to work to hone the talents and skills you were born with, but it's never a struggle to use these gifts.

**Purpose:** the work you use your gifts to do. Your purpose isn't about you. It's how you can serve others. Your purpose provides a way for you to use your gifts to connect with the marketplace and have a positive impact.

**Calling:** a pull in the direction you should go; the manner in which you fulfill your purpose. This pull doesn't even start until you acknowledge your gifts and chase your purpose.

People often tell me the tagline for Redefining Wealth, "Where we chase purpose, not money," is easy for me to say because I already have money. However, I was chasing purpose even when I was sleeping on my brother's couch. I knew anything I built without purpose wouldn't produce the results I wanted for the people I served or for me and my family. I turned down many opportunities that would've paid me well, but which didn't align with my purpose. I'm not here to tell you to quit your job because your job may very well be your purpose. I'm here to encourage you to work your way into your purpose no matter where it is. Begin by identifying and accepting it.

## 78. HONOR YOUR GIFTS

It's easy to see your gifts as unimpressive because they come easily to you. However, when you realize those same skills don't come easily to everyone else, you start to see the value of your gift. If you can open any refrigerator and imagine ten different meals made from the contents, you have a gift I don't have. If your poetry moves people to tears, you can turn a two-sentence idea into a great screenplay, or you can listen to a car engine and diagnose what's wrong with it, you have gifts I didn't receive. Most people can't do those things, and all those gifts have value. No matter what you're good at, there are thousands and thousands of people who don't have your gifts and wish they did.

As a child, I often got into trouble for talking too much, so I didn't grow up thinking I could make a living with my gift for communication. Even when I saw other speakers, I didn't quite connect the dots to a career path. It wasn't until I heard DeVon Franklin speak during my freshman year at USC that I realized I might have a gift for speaking. DeVon, who has since gone on to become a renowned speaker, was a college senior at the time, but he was so captivating from the stage. Listening to him, I thought I'd like to do the same thing one day.

As I built my real estate and mortgage business, I started speaking about home ownership, debt elimination, and other personal finance topics. I honored my gift by investing the time to develop it and using it as a tool to serve people. Most of the time, I didn't get paid to speak, but I attracted new clients, and following my gift led me to where I am now. Today, I often speak to audiences of thousands of people. That didn't happen overnight. It happened over more than a decade of honoring the same gift well-meaning people once told me was a liability.

I was using my gift when I talked too much in class as a child. I was just using it at the wrong time and in the wrong place. If your gifts are underappreciated where you are, it can cause you to question whether or not they're really gifts at all. However, you may be using the right gifts in the wrong industry, the wrong ministry, or the wrong environment. If your gifts are unfairly exploited, underappreciated, or misused, consider taking them elsewhere.

If your gifts are underutilized in your current work, you may be able transfer to a department more suited to what you can contribute. You may need to look for a totally different line of work with a different company, or you may decide entrepreneurship is the best way to make the most of your gifts. Those gifts make it possible for you to fulfill your purpose, but only if you honor them by putting them to good use.

*Redefine Wealth for Yourself*
Answer the following questions to identify your gifts. Consider how you can use those gifts in the work you do today or other work you feel called to do.

1. What came easily to you in childhood?
2. What projects do other people come to you for help with or advice about?
3. Which skills energize you when you use them?
4. What work gives you the most satisfaction?
5. What are you so happy doing that time flies by while you're engaged in it?

## 79. DON'T FOLLOW PASSION

Passions and gifts are not created equal. You can be extremely passionate about something, but that doesn't mean it's your gift. You can be passionate about a thing and not be very good at it at all. Many experts have said some version of "Follow your passion and the money will come," but I've found that to be hogwash. I feel obliged to disabuse as many people as possible of this ridiculous notion. It makes perfect sense when your passion and gifts are in alignment, but that's not always the case. When it's not, lifetimes are wasted chasing dreams that will never come true.

Most of us know at least one person who has spent decades chasing a dream while their family scrounges to pay the bills. That dream creates nothing of value except a little entertainment for the person pursuing it. Look at the man who spends thirty years trying to become a successful rapper. He's passionate about music, his lyrics, and the industry. However, if he doesn't have any gifts when it comes to rapping, his entire career will be an uphill battle. No matter how much passion he has, he's at a complete disadvantage, competing against young men and women who spit rhymes in their sleep.

There's nothing wrong with passion projects or undertakings you pursue for pure enjoyment, but don't expect to profit from them. Follow your gifts to find your purpose and your life's work. Don't try to force a purpose or pursuit unsuited to your natural abilities. Instead, show gratitude for the gifts and talents you were given, and allow them to lead you to your purposeful work.

### Redefine Wealth for Yourself

Fold a sheet of paper in half. On one side, list all the work, causes, groups of people, and issues that interest you. Circle three or four you feel the most passionate about. On the other side, make a list of the things that come easily to you. Circle two or three of your greatest strengths. Open the paper and consider which of your passions are supported by your gifts.

## 80. ANSWER THE CALL

When Sharon (not her real name) joined me for a breakthrough call, she'd worked in the beauty industry for thirteen years. For the last four of those years, she'd owned a salon, but it had never turned a profit. In fact, she was spending money to keep it going. Sharon wanted to get out of the salon and start a new business, but when I asked what she wanted to do, she gave me a list of things she wasn't good at doing.

When I pressed her, Sharon said she should probably go into real estate. She then listed five more business ideas, none related to the others, which she might want to pursue. She also mentioned something about her interest in art, but quickly brushed over it. When she was done, I asked her to tell me more about how art fit into her life, and she told me it was something that came naturally to her. She'd started dabbling four years earlier and was completely self-taught.

On her Instagram page, I found original artwork so outstanding I would've commissioned a work from her on the spot. "Why aren't you seriously pursuing this?" I asked her, and she explained running the salon took up all her time. Besides, she didn't want to be a "starving artist."

Art is subjective. It's worth as much as someone's willing to pay for it, but Sharon had serious limiting beliefs around how much income she could earn with her gift. We talked about shifting her mindset, and I advised her to sell a few pieces and use those sales to establish her prices going forward. My goal was to give her permission to choose her own beliefs about what it would mean to be a wealthy artist. I wanted her to see she could follow her gift to her purpose.

The Bible says many are called but few are chosen because we have the free will to choose to answer the call or not. The choosing must go both ways. Every day, I meet people with tremendous gifts and talents who refuse to answer the call on their lives, usually because it requires stepping into the unknown and facing the unfamiliar. Then they complain about people with less talent who are more successful. Those successful people may not be the best in the world at what they do, but they're willing to step out and do it.

If people can benefit from your gift, it has value. When people continually seek you out for your gift, it's a calling. Whether they're talking to you in person, hitting you up in your DMs, or actually picking up the phone to call you, it's a calling on your life. Don't relegate your greatest talent to be a hobby or side interest. You were given that gift for a reason. It's meant to support your life's work. This is your call to purpose. Answer the call.

### Redefine Wealth for Yourself

Does your work allow you to utilize your natural talents? If not, what's keeping you from choosing work that makes the most of your God-given gifts? Challenge the limiting beliefs holding you back and find or create work to put your gifts to good use. Do the work you're called to do.

## 81. DEFINE YOUR PURPOSE

In my programs and in the Redefining Wealth Facebook community, I hear from a lot of attorneys who feel trapped by their law practice. Some think going to law school was a mistake. Others are burnt out in the area of law they've chosen. One woman told me she'd always believed her purpose was tied to the law, and since she didn't want to practice any longer, she was worried she'd wasted all those years of her life.

Nothing ever has to be wasted. If your work is out of alignment with your purpose, consider it a stepping stone. Use what you've learned as you step into your purpose. Take the lessons, insights, and credibility your work has given you, apply them to the work you were purposed to do, and expect to be fairly compensated for it.

If your purpose involves charitable work, please don't think that makes money a non-factor. Any nonprofit has two audiences: the community it serves and the people who contribute to the nonprofit and make it possible for the work to be done. If you're running a nonprofit organization your purpose still has to be monetized in some way. It has to cover expenses like the salaries for the people running the organization, including you.

There's always a potential for financial gain connected to your purpose, and recognizing this truth is essential to creating wealth. If a pursuit can't sustain your lifestyle while blessing other people, it might be a passion, but it's probably not a purpose. You may have to think differently and remove some limiting beliefs to figure out how to work in your purpose and earn more money, but it's always possible.

Having a clear purpose statement will keep you on track and prevent you from being distracted or dissuaded from your purpose. My current purpose statement reads: "My purpose is to lead people to live their life's purpose, find fulfillment, and earn more without chasing money." Everything I do in my work has to serve that purpose. Anything that doesn't won't make it on my work calendar.

As you develop your purpose statement, don't become too married to it. Purpose evolves and so will your purpose statement, but if you follow it and operate in your purpose, you'll never have to chase money. Everything you create, every job you accept, every project you take on should be in alignment with your purpose statement. You can have other passions, but follow them in your free time. Treat them as hobbies and invest most of your resources in chasing your purpose.

### Redefine Wealth for Yourself

Think through the following questions, and based on your answers, write out your purpose statement. Keep it where you can read it often.

1. Who are you called to serve?
2. How will you serve them?
3. What positive impact do you want to have on their lives?
4. How will you use your gifts to fulfill your purpose?

## 82. FOCUS ON YOUR UNFAIR ADVANTAGE

For four years, my segment on the Steve Harvey radio show allowed me to talk to millions of listeners around the country about money. It was only a quick four minutes on air, but I spent hours each week scouring emails to find questions to answer on subjects that would serve most of the people listening and recording thoughtful responses. It was worth the effort, but over time, I wanted to talk about more than money. I wanted to talk about real wealth. I wanted to talk about decluttering, and relationships, and mental fitness, but I had to work hard to connect everything directly back to money to stay on message with the theme of my segment.

Once I launched my podcast, I was torn between the podcast, where I could share my message exactly as I wanted to share it, and the radio show, which put me in front of more people. Seven months in, I could see I was on to something with *Redefining Wealth*. I certainly didn't have the listener numbers the radio show had, but I was growing consistently. The radio show had blessed me with opportunities and recognition, but I had to fight to include more of the conversation I wanted to have with my audience. I prayed for guidance, and I realized I was holding on to the platform at the cost of going all in with where my purpose was taking me. That season of my life had been wonderful, but it was time to bring it to a close, and in 2018, I ended my segment on the radio show.

Almost as soon as I left, new opportunities opened up for me. My podcast continued to grow, and all of a sudden, mainstream media could see me. I discovered I'd been pigeon-holed as a "Black" expert for some time because of my affiliation with the show, but on the podcast, I was just the expert, and I was able to attract a wider audience. As the podcast took off and opened more doors for me, I looked back with appreciation at my time on the radio show because it had given me an unfair advantage in the podcasting world.

I'd spent four years recording segments on my own, talking to the ether, and I learned to do it with passion and enthusiasm, so I could keep listeners engaged. When I launched the podcast, I thought it would be hard to talk to an audience I couldn't see and who wasn't listening live for forty-five minutes, but it turned out to be easy for me. I'd learned how to talk to no one by doing the radio show, and I'd learned how to carry a topic for up to an hour or more from speaking on the stage. My unfair advantage—the advantage of having gifts and experiences in a combination other podcasters didn't have—put me ahead of the game.

There are bloggers who know how to crank out a thousand words a day like it's nothing. There are internet marketers who have an instinct for peppering their websites with affiliate links to bring in six figures in a month. I could try to mimic what they do, but I have no advantage in those areas. I have no experience or gifts to help me do well, and I have no desire to try to compete with someone else's unfair advantage.

Honing in on your own unfair competitive advantage can make it easier for you to accept and fulfill your purpose. The combination of your gifts and the experiences that have allowed you to develop those gifts in unique ways positions you to pursue your purpose like nobody else can. Don't waste your time fighting to do the things you're *kind of* good at doing. Focus on your unfair advantage and employ it to live your purpose.

> ### Redefine Wealth for Yourself
> Make a list of your gifts and a list of the experiences that have allowed you to develop your gifts in different ways. Identify your unfair advantage and look for ways to use it to fulfill your purpose.

## 83. TEST YOUR FULFILLMENT

By the time I got off the 405 freeway and onto Long Beach Boulevard, the tears had started to fall. As I got closer to the office, my stomach twisted into knots. I parked in the parking lot and picked up my cell phone. My mom prayed for me for ten minutes while I cried hysterically. Finally, I put on some gospel music to try to pump myself up, took a deep breath, and went to work. I got through the morning by looking forward to lunchtime when I got out of the office as fast as I could. I went shopping, mindlessly spending to forget about my job for that brief hour. I got through the last half of the day by counting down to five o'clock, when I'd be free.

The same scene played out every day while I worked with a woman with whom I didn't share core values. Working with her made it hard for me to honor my values every day, and I was extremely unhappy. As miserable as I was, I wasn't yet wise enough to realize what a dangerous place I was in. When my cousin, also in her twenties, passed away from stress-related conditions, I finally woke up. She'd gone to a job she hated for years, and it had likely contributed to her untimely death. Not long after that, I left the business.

Most of us spend more time working than we do anything else. If your work doesn't give you peace and joy, if you don't get goose-bumps anymore when you think about work, if you don't feel the same level of excitement you had when you were dating somebody new, it might be time for a change. Maybe you're not experiencing high blood pressure or anxiety related to your work, but are you enthusiastic and fulfilled?

A lack of fulfillment at work can show up in a variety of ways:

- You start every week looking forward to Friday.
- You constantly complain about your job.
- You're physically or mentally exhausted during the work week, but fine on the weekends.
- You portray yourself as happy with your work on social media, but secretly, you're bored, weary, or frustrated.
- You need a drink or make poor food choices to relax after a long day of work.
- You indulge in excessive shopping to forget about your work.

Whatever symptoms manifest for you when you're unfulfilled at work, there's a void in your life. You're not operating in your gifts and your unfair advantage is underutilized. Your job is out of alignment with your core values. There's a void because you're so far out of your purpose. When we look at our definition of wealth as wellbeing, it's clear your work is about so much more than your paycheck. Not everyone needs to make a million dollars a year to be happy and ful-filled in their work. Instead of focusing on the dollars, live your life's purpose and focus on fulfillment, and opportunities will steadily fall into place.

## *Redefine Wealth for Yourself*

Test your fulfillment by responding true or false to the following statements. If you have more than one false, use the previous principles in this chapter to figure out how you can become more fulfilled in your work or move on to work better suited to your gifts, your purpose, and your calling.

1. I look forward to going to work on most days.
2. My work gives me energy.
3. The words I speak about my work are positive most of the time.
4. My work makes the most of my gifts.
5. I positively impact other people through my work.
6. Even when I'm not at work, ideas for my work flow easily to me.
7. Most of what I do at work comes naturally to me.
8. I love what I do and who I do it with and for.

## CHAPTER 14

# Put Purpose to Work

I DIDN'T KNOW EXACTLY how I would do it, but as I rebuilt my financial life in the middle of the Great Recession, I wanted to take as many people with me as possible. My purpose was clear, but I didn't have a poetic way to talk to people about how to seek wisdom and find wealth. I didn't have a platform yet. I didn't have a job, much less a position in alignment with my purpose.

To kick-start my efforts, I launched a free BlogSpot blog with the tagline "Because becoming wealthy has 100% nothing to do with money." At the time, I had very little knowledge about the internet or online business. I built an ugly website and blogged about the basics of personal finance. My first website still lives on the world wide web because I have no idea what the password is or how to shut down the account. My blog was a humble beginning, but over time, it allowed me to reach people and served as a platform for my purpose.

My audience was made up of people like me and those a few steps behind me. They didn't care how unpolished my website looked. They didn't need me to be earning seven figures. All they wanted was information they could apply to get results at a time when unemployment and foreclosure rates were higher than they'd been in our lifetime. I gave them strategies to live a wealthy life. I hadn't yet articulated the root of wealth as wellbeing, but in addition to money, I talked about relationships, spirituality, gratitude, and health. Over the years, those topics evolved into the Six Pillars of Wealth, the foundation for my current business.

No one paid me to teach them about money in the beginning, but I was fulfilling my purpose. In the following months and years, I found new ways to share my message, in articles, and videos, and as a volunteer. It took time and consistent effort, but eventually, I reached a point where I got paid to do what I loved.

As you recognize and accept your purpose, there comes a time when you have to take action and put your purpose to work. Knowing your purpose isn't enough. You have to live it.

## 84. DEFINE YOUR CORE VALUES

During my childhood, my single mom worked twelve-hour shifts and commuted an hour and a half each way. Because her job was so demanding, my grandmother basically raised me, but my grandmother didn't drive and wasn't comfortable speaking to Americans in a formal capacity, so she wasn't able to contribute to my education or extracurricular activities. Although I attended the same school from fifth grade to twelfth grade, I could count on one hand the number of times my mother came to my school, and two of those were when I was suspended for fighting. I was a true latchkey kid, and I often depended on other people for rides. Those angels went out of their way to take me from school back home to the hood. They invested in a smart, ambitious, hardworking little girl, and transported me when my mother had to work ninety-seven percent of the time.

Unlike my mother, my father had a lot of flexibility in his life. When I played sports, he showed up for several of my games, something my mother couldn't do. He didn't have a long commute taking up hours of his day. When it was time for me to receive my allowance, my grandmother and I walked to my father's store, so I knew where he worked.

179

However, I had no clue what he did for a living. One day, we had dinner at Red Lobster, and I asked him, "What's your job? Why can you come to my school things when my mom can't?" My father replied, "I make my own schedule. I do what I want to do because I'm an entrepreneur."

While I grew to respect my mom's sacrifice, entrepreneur sounded much more appealing than what she did for a living. She was tied to the schedule someone else dictated, and my dad had time on his hands. My mom drove a Camry while he drove a Benz. As hard as she worked, we still lived in the hood. Sitting across the table from my father, I decided I would be an entrepreneur too. The material rewards looked enticing, but the freedom appealed to me even more. I wanted to be a mom one day, and I wanted the flexibility to attend my child's school plays, parent-teacher conferences, games, and events.

Flexibility became a core value for me back then and it still is. As an entrepreneur, like my father, I create my own schedule and manage my day as I see fit. My business allows me to schedule things around my daughter's needs. Since she was five years old, I've worked from my home office, and I'm free to visit her school or attend her events whenever I want.

Whether you run your own business or work for yourself, to put your purpose to work you must honor your values, and that means you have to identify them. If you're not one hundred percent sure of your core values, reflect on the lessons you've learned from different seasons of your life. Identify common themes. Your core values are likely things you recognized as important from an early age. Think about the person you want to be. Imagine how you want other people to describe you. These descriptors are likely your core values. Once you define them, protect them. Require the people in your life to honor those values, and most of all, require it of yourself.

*Redefine Wealth for Yourself*
Write your answers to the following questions to clarify your core values.

1. What matters most in your life?
2. What are the greatest lessons you've learned so far in your lifetime?
3. What lessons have you seen play out many times in different ways?
4. What are the most important qualities in a close friend or colleague?
5. What kind of person do you want to be?
6. How do you want other people to describe you?
7. Create a list of five to seven values that mean the most to you and make decisions in alignment with those values as you put purpose to work.

# 85. CRAFT YOUR DREAM CAREER

While I was out of work in 2010, I sat, I sat down and wrote in my journal a description of my ideal job. I detailed a position in which I'd be paid to teach people the basics of personal finance. I described the audience I'd serve and how I'd travel to churches and other organizations to meet people where they were and teach them how to make the most of their money. It would be, I thought, my dream career.

Around this time, I started volunteering for the nonprofit organization I mentioned in an earlier chapter. Since I didn't have a job, I worked with them almost every week. Whenever I received an email soliciting volunteers, I signed up because it allowed me to do the work of teaching personal finance. They didn't pay me, but they gave me an opportunity to work in my purpose.

One day, I received a phone call from the local head of the organization. A new position had opened within the organization, and he suggested I apply for it. The job description read like someone had copied my description of my ideal job straight from my journal. I applied for and landed the job and stepped into my dream career, earning $2400 a month, which was a blessing when my most recent employment had netted me $500 every two weeks. Besides, I was able to help people achieve their financial goals. I was walking in my purpose.

Because I had a clear picture of the work I wanted to do, I easily recognized the right job for me when it came along. Even before there was an official position, I got closer to my dream career through my volunteer work. My experience isn't exceptional. Your dream career is possible for you too. The work you do now doesn't have to be the work you always do. If the job you want doesn't yet exist, you can make it a reality. Figure out what it will look like, and then craft your dream career.

### Redesign Wealth for Yourself

Write your own dream job description. Do you work for yourself or someone else? How do you put your purpose to work every day? Who do you serve? How do you serve them? What will you achieve? Keep your dream career in mind as you seek new opportunities.

## 86. DESIGN YOUR IDEAL DAY

While my work with the nonprofit organization suited my purpose perfectly, it wasn't long before I grew frustrated with the rules and routines of office work. Despite my circumstances, I never lost sight of the decision I made, that day in Red Lobster with my dad, to become an entrepreneur. My day started with leaving home at seven in the morning to drop off Reagan at preschool and fighting Atlanta traffic to drop off my niece, who lived with us, at her high school on the other side of town. Then, I drove to various suburbs of Atlanta to give workshops. At the end of the day, my employer expected me to return to our office in the heart of the city to drop off paperwork before I made the trek back to our suburb in the middle of rush hour traffic.

I hated running late every day to pick up Reagan from preschool. More than that, it burned me up that my supervisor felt like I had to be in the office during certain hours, even if my work was done or I could easily finish it from home. I never needed to be micromanaged, and I pushed back against it.

I forgot to include the details of how my work would fit into my life when I crafted my "dream job." Yes, I wanted to teach people about personal finance, but not at the cost of time with my family or peace of mind. My core value of flexibility wasn't being honored, so I kept my dream career description, but I also wrote a description of my ideal day. It read something like the following:

> *I wake up in the morning and pray and meditate before my family gets up. I take my daughter to school and then return to my house, where I make my coffee with my favorite vanilla creamer. Wearing my fuzzy slippers, I walk down to my home office. I coach people over the phone and have plenty of time to write blog posts, articles, and books. I dress up when I want to, not because I have to. At the end of the day, I pick up my daughter from school on time.*

That was what I wanted back in 2010, and it's essentially the way I live my life now. I've done this exercise multiple times over the years, and each time, I got more clarity about how I want to live my life while I work in my purpose. I've worked from home for a decade, but I didn't have my ideal day right away. I incorporated one element at a time until my vision became my reality.

It's essential to understand the kind of work you want to do as you chase purpose instead of money. However, it's just as important to have a clear picture of what your days will look like. Designing your ideal day, requires you to consider all the pillars—FIT, PEOPLE, SPACE, FAITH, WORK, and MONEY. Keep refining your model until you have a picture of harmony among all the pillars.

Your ideal day may differ completely from mine. Maybe you don't have children to drive to school. Perhaps you really love the energy you get from working with other people in a shared office space. Maybe you prefer more time for your faith practices at the end of the day. Define your ideal day for yourself. That's the only way you'll ever come close to creating it.

*Redefine Wealth for Yourself*
It's your turn. Write a description of your ideal day, starting from the moment you wake up and ending when you turn in for the night. Include as much detail as possible and revisit this document periodically to assess what you've implemented and what you might want to change.

Here are a few questions to get you started:

1. Where do you wake up? What kind of home is it? Where is it located?
2. Who's in your home with you?
3. How do you dress for the day?
4. How do you spend your morning?
5. What kind of work do you do?
6. Where do you work?
7. How does your work serve your purpose?
8. When and how do you end your work day?
9. What do your evenings look like?
10. What's your nighttime routine?

# 87. SPEAK YOUR DREAMS

"So what do you do?"

Stop and think before you answer that question. Whether you're networking, attending a conference, or meeting people at a dinner party, your occupation is usually one of the first things new people want to know about you. Some people recoil from the question. They want to be seen as more than their work, but when you're working in your purpose, what you do is more than a job. It's integral to your life and to you as a person. Even if you haven't officially launched your business or landed your dream job yet, start answering this question with the work you're called to do. Start telling people about your purpose.

When I worked for the nonprofit organization, I spoke and gave workshops as a part of my job. When I posted on social media about those events, I tagged the nonprofit, but I didn't describe myself as an employee. I described myself as a speaker. At events, I introduced myself as a money expert, a speaker, and the author of a forthcoming book on personal finance. I was those things, so I spoke about them as part of who I was, not as a part of a job. Because of this, people thought of me not as an employee, but as a speaker, author, and expert. In fact, when I finally announced I was leaving my day job to build my business, many people were shocked. It had never occurred to them that I worked for someone else.

Often, people I meet introduce themselves by telling me how long they've been trapped in their day job and why they hate working there. Then, they finally mention their purpose, almost as an afterthought. When the conversation is over, all I can remember is what they don't like about their work. This doesn't leave a favorable impression.

If you want a new job, stop talking about the one you have now. Focus on what you want more of in your work. If you work for the city, but you want to be an event planner, introduce yourself as someone who helps people plan exceptional, elegant events. Speak life into your dream. You never know if the person listening has the power to bless you directly or indirectly. Give them something to work with.

Obviously, if you're representing your employer at a work event, you need to mention your position. However, you don't have to lead with that outside of the scope of your job. Once you've identified your dream career, you'll get there a lot faster by changing the narrative of your work to align with that career. Stop complaining about your job and start introducing yourself as what you want to be known for doing.

When I interviewed Billionaire PA on the podcast, he talked about how important it is to speak your dreams out loud. I grew up believing people would steal your ideas if you shared your dream, and that limiting belief paralyzed me in some ways. My fear kept me from seeking wisdom when I should have. People can't steal your dream, but they can't help you with it if they don't know about it either. Talk about your dream as if it's already yours, and you'll make it a reality much faster.

> ### *Redefine Wealth for Yourself*
> Practice telling people what you do by sharing your dream. Post about it on social media, and when you meet people, introduce yourself as what you expect to be. Don't make false claims, but tell people about the product or service you provide or have forthcoming and become who you say you are.

## 88. ANNIHILATE EXCUSES

One of my coaching clients came to our Power Hour wearing a hijab. She identified as Muslim, and when I asked her to describe her clients, she said they were also Muslim. However, when I suggested she target Muslims in her sales copy, she resisted. No one else was paying her for her services, but she didn't want to be "limited" to speaking to Muslims.

I explained that targeting a specific audience wouldn't prevent anyone else from hiring her, but she had an opportunity to connect with a niche not everyone could reach in an authentic way. Still, she resisted. Whatever suggestion I made, she had an excuse as to why she couldn't do it, why it wasn't a good idea, or why it wouldn't work for her. I believe she implemented very few of my suggestions, and more than likely, she continued to struggle to make progress in her business.

We all have limiting beliefs, the stories we tell ourselves about why we can't do something we want or need to do. For years, I told myself I was bad with technology. Even as software became more user-friendly and accessible, I held on to that excuse. Many times, I found myself hamstrung because I needed to get something done on my website or a sales page but my tech specialist wasn't available. When I finally decided to seek a solution I could manage without a support team, a friend told me about a new option. I tried it, and lo and behold, I set up everything for my upcoming launch all on my own.

Being bad at tech had been an excuse for me to avoid learning anything about those systems for way too long. I'd also bought into the idea that my time was better spent working in my zone of genius than setting up tech. While that's true to an extent, it wasn't an excuse to avoid learning about technology. Yes, I can hire someone to do the work, but I also need to understand it. Letting go of my limiting beliefs around technology freed me to have more hands-on control in my business when I need it, and as a byproduct of being able to launch without always waiting for other people, we've generated more revenue.

Over the years, I've heard every excuse for why people can't work in their purpose. I don't have time. No one will hire me. I don't have the right degrees or certificates. I can't afford to launch a business. The course I need is too expensive. I don't learn well online, and I can't find an in-person workshop. The list of excuses is endless, but you have to start somewhere.

If you think you don't have time to put your purpose to work, go back to the SPACE pillar and take steps to create more time in your life. If you can't afford the course you need, buy a how-to book or check one out of the library. If no one will give you the job you want, figure out how to create it or find a place to volunteer until you figure out your next step. There's always a way to put your purpose to work.

### Redefine Wealth for Yourself

If excuses are stopping you from putting your purpose to work, go back to the FIT pillar (Chapter 2: Develop a Fit Mindset), and do the necessary mindset work to let go of those limiting beliefs.

## 89. TAKE THE NEXT BEST STEP

Traci Burton joined Purpose to Platform at twenty-five years old with a mission to help children with literacy. However, when she couldn't figure out how to make that financially fruitful, Tracey switched gears. On a coaching call, she wanted to know how to launch a T-shirt business. I advised her to stay focused on her purpose, but starting a t-shirt business seemed so much easier to her. She knew how to set up a sales cart, order custom T-shirts, and promote her business on social media. But she had no idea how to profit while having a positive impact on children's literacy. "I'm trying to get to the cash," she explained.

"But is that purposeful?" I asked her. "Is it what you said you want to do? Just take the next best step. You don't have to see the whole plan."

Traci took the next best step toward working in her purpose by going through the modules in the program. She did the homework and came to understand why she had such a heart for children's literacy. Then, she did the next best thing and the next, week after week. She got funding for a rap video about literacy. The local newspaper featured her efforts, and she was offered space to do her literacy work. The governor of her state recognized her for her work, and early in 2020, she was contacted by *Time* magazine to be featured as an urban missionary.

I could never have promised Traci her work would lead to an appearance in a prominent national magazine or recognition from the governor. I couldn't see that part of the big picture and neither could she, but because she stayed focused on her purpose and took consistent action, her work took her to places she hadn't imagined. When you take the next best step, you give God something to bless, and you give people something to support.

If you don't know what to do next, your next step is research, taking a course, or joining a program to help you figure it out. There's always a way to move closer to your purpose. You don't have to see the whole plan, just take the next best step.

### *Redefine Wealth for Yourself*
Figure out the next best step to work in your purpose and take it.

## CHAPTER 15

# Earn More Without Chasing

WHEN I WORKED for the nonprofit, many of clients came in looking for ways to cut expenses and save money. Many of these people were economically disadvantaged and had already cut their spending to the bone. They were couponing and brown-bagging their lunch every day. They told their kids, "no," when they asked for simple pleasures. Bigger expenses, like summer camps or family vacations, were out of the question.

When Lara (not her real name) came in for financial counseling, she was in a similar position. A single mom residing in low-income housing, she wanted to know how to spend less money. She was accustomed to people telling her to cut back on her lifestyle, but she didn't have much left to give up. Instead of telling her how to spend less, I asked Lara, "What about earning more money instead?"

My clients had limiting beliefs around money, and much of the personal finance industry fed into those beliefs. Popular money experts sent the message that the only way to get ahead was to spend less, but I had a different perspective. I wanted my clients to figure out how to earn more money so they could raise the level of their lifestyle in ways that mattered to them. To that end, I encouraged them to incorporate entrepreneurship into their income-producing activities.

Many of these people knew how to hustle; they braided hair or sold t-shirts to make a little money on the side. They had the potential to create real income from those skills, but they didn't know where to start. They'd fallen for the myth that it takes a lot of money to make money, but they weren't setting out to launch seven-figure businesses. They just needed to earn enough to get out of survival mode, which they could do with little or no start-up capital.

Lara had a gift for turning plain ceramic items, like mugs and vases, into unique gifts, and when I suggested she sell those items, she was open to the idea. It simply hadn't occurred to her that she could earn a substantial income doing something she enjoyed rather than running after hustles that promised extra income but took her away from her kids and boxed her into work she didn't like. Instead of chasing money, she could work in her gift and earn more.

Lara came in to use our computers to set up her products to sell online. She found ceramic pieces at craft stores and dollar stores. Using her natural abilities, she turned $15 or $20 at a time into $100, and then she used a percentage of her profits to purchase more inventory. Soon, she was earning enough to make a material difference in her life. She no longer felt the pressure of figuring out how she would make ends meet every month. Lara discovered her gifts had value.

Too many people scramble to figure out how to stretch their paycheck just a bit further while, the gifts that could help them earn more lie dormant. Put to use in an entrepreneurial venture, those gifts could mean the difference between struggling to get by and having more than enough. Admittedly, I'm biased toward business ownership as a means to earn more without ever chasing money. That bias, however, is based on my personal experience and my experience coaching hundreds of people to achieve their financial goals. Whether you go all in or have a business on the side while you work your nine-to-five, entrepreneurship multiplies your ability to increase your income.

## 90. EMPIRE YOUR IDEAS

Gerald and I were driving one day when he came up with the idea for his book, *Don't Just Start a Business; Build an Empire*. At the heart of the book is the idea that people who work fall into one of three categories. These categories aren't just the roles you play. They're the mindsets you bring to any work you do.

The three work mindsets are:

1. Employee
2. Entrepreneur
3. Empire builder

People with an employee mindset prioritize the feeling of security they get from a job. They shy away from the unknown and prefer to execute directives rather than own responsibility for setting the direction. When they're high performers, employees are valuable team members for business owners. The vast majority of people have an employee mindset.

An entrepreneur mindset requires recognition that you can create something of value on your own and the desire to do so. Even when they work for someone else, people with an entrepreneur mindset take initiative and take on some risk. When they go out on their own to build a business, they do what it takes to compete in the marketplace, but they stop there. Whatever business they create requires their presence to function, and their business structure limits what they can earn.

And then there are the empire builders. These people are willing to take bigger risks, innovate, and change the game for everyone else in their industry. Empire builders understand there are no ceilings on the income they can create or the positive impact they can have on the world. They create diverse streams of income and work towards a goal of no longer trading dollars for hours. Empire builders create something of value while building an enterprise which can function even if they step away.

There's nothing wrong with being an employee. Employees are the lifeblood of many businesses. And entrepreneurs run many of the businesses we all love to frequent. Your favorite local restaurant, salon, barbershop, and coffee shop are all likely run by entrepreneurs. Many of these business owners are content with what they've created. However, if you want to maximize your ability to earn more money without chasing, you have to shift to think like an empire builder. Remove any limits you have on what you can do with your ideas. Leverage your resources to create multiple streams of income and, in the process, serve many more people as you build your empire.

> ### Redefine Wealth for Yourself
> Write out at least twenty ways you can earn more and positively impact more people by following your purpose. Don't try to implement all these ideas at once. Instead, begin to think like an empire builder so you can recognize opportunities to create a sustainable business that fulfills your purpose and maximizes your income.

## 91. RELEASE YOUR GENIUS

A few years ago, I connected with a business owner who was brilliant at what he did. He was surrounded by people who wanted what he had to offer, and he had plenty of support from his mastermind and other smart, successful people in his circle. I waited for him to launch the program he was developing because my community could have benefited from it. I would have promoted it, but I'm still waiting. Since the time he and I met, I've launched Purpose 2 Platform and Command the Stage, and Podcast with Purpose, and I've made hundreds of thousands of dollars by serving my clients in those programs.

I gave myself ninety days to launch Purpose 2 Platform, and we had a sloppy launch because I was still figuring out some of the technology. Command the Stage didn't happen the way I'd planned either. Because of the COVID-19 pandemic, we had to take our live program virtual. Even with those imperfections, the women in both programs sent me dozens of testimonials sharing how they benefited and how glad they were to have participated.

As I write this, the other business owner still hasn't released anything. He has an audience, and he has valuable knowledge. But he can't seem to bring himself to put something out in the world. I can only speculate about what's holding him back, but a good guess is that it goes back to the FIT pillar and his mindset. From what I can see, the only things standing between him and a successful launch is him. If you're in a similar position—you have an idea for a product or service, but you can never seem to launch—go back to Chapter 2 and develop your mindset to put your ideas out into the world.

When you refuse to release your genius because you're afraid you'll fail, afraid of what people will say, or afraid no one will buy your offer, you cheat yourself of the opportunity to learn more and to earn more. Stop trying to get it just right. Make it good enough and put it out there. Get feedback and make changes after you launch, but don't rob other people of what they're waiting to get from you. Release your genius so you can profit and they can benefit from your knowledge.

### Redefine Wealth for Yourself

Do you have an idea for a product or service to fulfill your purpose and earn more money at the same time? Make a list of everything you need to do to make it possible for people to give you money in exchange for the value your product or service provides. Find the help you need to get started and commit to releasing your genius.

## 92. DELEGATE DECISIVELY

When I met with my client, an attorney named Grace (not her real name), for a coaching session, she explained that she was too busy to work on her business. She blocked time on her calendar, but each week, she ended up with a list of unfinished tasks and projects, like building her website, writing her book, and billing clients. Even after we went through the exercise of removing unnecessary activities from her calendar, she didn't have time to do it all. Grace had one big problem with her schedule. She was trying to do everything on her own.

It was clear Grace needed to learn to delegate, and I suggested she start by delegating one small thing. She agreed to use an app for grocery shopping and delivery. For her, it was worth the cost to have someone else drive to the store, walk the aisles, make sure they got everything on the list, stand in line to check out, and drive to her house with the week's supply of food. Grace decided to pay someone to grocery shop so she could spend those three or four hours working on her business or enjoying her family.

The 80/20 rule, also known as the Pareto Principle, suggests that eighty percent of the results you create come from just twenty percent of your efforts. That means most people create eighty percent of their material wealth with just twenty percent of their efforts. The other eighty percent of their work time and energy goes into tasks which don't directly contribute to the bottom line. Take the example of a professional speaker. She spends just twenty percent of her time preparing to speak and speaking from the stage. The other eighty percent of the time she maintains her website, writes emails, posts on social media, schedules travel, and invoices for her services. Only twenty percent of her time is spent where it really matters.

That doesn't mean the activities in that other eighty percent aren't important, but if you can delegate much of the eighty percent that falls outside of your lane of genius, you can spend more time working on the things that really matter. You can choose to spend more than twenty percent of your time honing and applying your craft, improving your professional skills, and doing the work that gets you results. When you spend more time working in your lane of genius—the work you do best, the things no one else can do quite like you—you earn more without working more.

Having an assistant has allowed me to develop more mastery in the skills that make a material difference to my business. As I speak more, coach more, and record more podcasts, I improve in those areas. I could spend my time doing the administrative work my assistant does, but it wouldn't help me or my business grow.

By delegating, you not only get to spend more time in your lane of genius, you also give someone else the opportunity to do the same. The person shopping for your groceries might just love the experience of being in the grocery store. The ten hours of work you give a virtual assistant every week could be her chance to earn money with skills she spent years developing. On the other hand, when you hold so tightly to your responsibilities and your money that you refuse to delegate anything, you cheat other people out of opportunities.

Lean into your strengths and hire to cover your weaknesses. Delegate tasks other people can handle as well as or better than you can. If you have a job and no one reports to you, delegate in other areas of your life, and free more of your time to develop your professional skills. If you're a solopreneur, hire a virtual assistant on a project basis or for a few hours a week or delegate tasks to freelancers and gig workers. There's always something you can delegate, and when you do, you'll have more time to use your gifts, do work you love, and earn more money.

### Redefine Wealth for Yourself

Take a look at the ways you spend work hours. Make a list of tasks you can delegate with the specific goal of freeing up more time to work in your strengths so you can earn more without chasing money. Choose one task to delegate today.

## 93. MASTER ONE THING

When I interviewed best-selling author and self-described serial entrepreneur Jordan Raynor, on the *Redefining Wealth* podcast, we talked about the importance of mastery. Jordan helps Christians do their most exceptional work for the glory of God and the good of others. He and I agreed you can be multi-passionate—most of us are multidimensional people with many interests—but you won't make real progress in any area when you're unfocused. "Most people make a millimeter of progress in a million different directions," Jordan said. "That's not mastery."

Jordan says he was "the quintessential jack of all trades and master of none" early in his career. He was good at a lot of things, but he wasn't world-class at any of them. He could embrace being a jack of all trades, but he wasn't happy being a master of none. Jordan wrote his book, *Master of One*, to share what he learned about how to find, focus on, and master the work you were created to do.

Jordan's believes becoming a master of your craft isn't a destination you can reach. It's a lifelong process. Experimentation and exploration will help you determine what's for you and what's not. He suggests you commit to one thing and eliminate everything else to begin the process of becoming a master of one. Fortunately, you don't have to completely give up your other interests. Often, you'll find several of your interests come together in some way. As you hone your skills and develop a level of excellence in one area, you can continually look for the thread that connects all your passions.

Don't use being multi-passionate as an excuse not to focus. Drill down on one thing. Master it and expand from there. Your one thing will be the foundation on which you can build or from which you can pivot to include many of your other interests.

### *Redefine Wealth for Yourself*

Commit to focusing on the one thing you want to master, to the exclusion of everything else, for a period of time. Strive for excellence in that one area before you try to be great in another.

## 94. NETWORK WITH INTENTION

Two weeks before I launched the *Redefining Wealth* podcast, I attended Podcast Movement, a huge conference for podcasters and podcast industry professionals. Before I went down to the first day's activities, I wrote out exactly what I needed from the event. I wanted to meet a podcast editor and find three people who would interview me on their podcasts in time for my launch.

I explained to anyone I talked to exactly what I wanted from the conference. One of the first people I met shared that there were live podcast recordings going on in a nearby room, and I ended up recording two podcasts while I was there. I was invited to be a guest on five more podcasts in the next couple of weeks, and I found a podcast editor who was able to start working with me the next weekend. I also met the founder of Repurpose.io, who told me about software he'd developed to market podcasts, and I started using it right away. I got everything I wanted from that event, and so much more.

One year later, I returned to Podcast Movement as a breakout speaker, and in my session, I shared how I'd gotten my first one hundred thousand downloads. The following year, I returned as a keynote speaker on the cusp of one million downloads. As I write this, the *Redefining Wealth* podcast has reached more than four million downloads as we celebrate our three-year anniversary. Much of that success came from the intentions I set and the actions I took around my participation in Podcast Movement. I can directly trace multiple five figures of income back to that event and it was all earned with ease and grace.

Entrepreneurs and professionals often treat networking like a card-collecting contest, and they're often shocked when I tell them I don't carry business cards, but let's be honest. Most of the cards handed out at an event end up in the bottom of a purse or desk drawer. When you're intentional about networking, business cards become unnecessary. With cell phones and social media, you can immediately follow or connect with people, schedule a meeting, or exchange cell phone numbers. You can forget about counting cards and focus on making connections that matter.

Many people are nervous about networking because they don't have a plan. Instead of looking to make meaningful connections, they hang out next to the appetizers and latch on to anyone willing to engage with them for the rest of the night. Or they spend their time talking about everything but the work they do, turning the event into a social activity and leaving no further along in their professional goals than they'd been when they arrived.

Before you buy a ticket or register to attend any event, decide to be intentional with your time. Before you walk through the door, ask yourself what you need to take your business or your career to the next level. Commit to asking at least three people what you can help them with and tell them what you need. Most people want to help if they can. If they know of a resource or opportunity that suits your needs, they'll tell you about it. Some people are natural connectors and will have already met people in the room who can help you and will make that introduction.

Be intentional about getting what you need, but be just as intentional about giving when you network. Giving is essential to living a wealthy life and helps you remember none of us build a business or career alone. If you can be a resource or make a helpful introduction, do it. What you give may never come back to you from the person you helped, but it will always come back to you sooner or later.

### Redefine Wealth for Yourself

Before you attend any event or networking opportunity, get clear on why you're going and make the most of the event with the following steps:

1. Write down two or three things you need to take the next steps in your business.
2. Write your intention to meet someone who can directly or indirectly assist you with those things.
3. Tell at least three people at the event what you need to take the next steps in your business or career.
4. Ask at least three people at the event, "How can I support you?"
5. Follow-up on meaningful connections and resources.

## 95. OBEDIENCE OVER PERFECTION

When she showed up in Command the Stage, my program for transformational speakers, Latoya Matthews wasn't ready to tell her story. She wanted to help women see beauty for ashes, and heal from the trauma, guilt, and shame of abortions, so they could move on with their lives and thrive. To do that, Latoya needed to share her own experience, but she talked around the heart of the issue. Finally, on our small group coaching call, I asked her what she was leaving out. She had enrolled in the program to learn to use her story to help people, but she couldn't connect with her intended audience until she was ready to share her full truth.

Latoya wasn't alone. So many of her cohorts in the program wanted to serve people with their without telling the stories they were being called to share. Fortunately, Latoya didn't take long to submit to the idea that, to pursue her purpose, she needed to tell her story. Once she did, she got immediate results. She was one of the few participants in the program to book podcast interviews before we were done. Before Command the Stage ended, she already had two clients, even though she hadn't polished her story to perfection, and within months, she filled her coaching program. Those podcast audiences and the clients who came on board didn't need her perfection. They needed her obedience and her willingness to tell her story and offer her help.

As a coach, I teach the women in my programs that work is about living your life's purpose. To live your purpose, you have to be obedient to what the Holy Spirit, the God your worship, or your intuition directs you to do. Obedience doesn't care about your feelings, your convenience, or your comfort. Obedience isn't all about you. It's about how you can live a life of fulfillment and be of service to other people.

The perfectionist in me often struggles to be obedient. Instinctively, I don't want to move forward until everything is perfect. I started to break free from that expectation in 2017. One day, on my way home from the gym, I got a download in my spirit. The message would be a blessing to someone if I went live on social media and delivered the message while it was fresh in my mind. However, I resisted. My workout wig was crooked, and my makeup wasn't done. I didn't want to go live until I cleaned up, but the message was slipping away from me.

And then I heard a still small voice ask, "So you think your makeup is more important than the message?"

I delayed my shower, put on some clothes, and walked down the hallway to my office, where I fired up my computer and went live. When I came back from showering, I had dozens of comments from people telling me the live broadcast was exactly what they needed to hear in that moment. My message had made a difference.

When you're called to do something, the most important part of the process is obedience. People have grace for your imperfections. If you want to be of value or you pray for God to use you, then you can't just take those opportunities when you're feeling cute. God promises us so many good things, but to get your blessings, your obedience is required.

Evangelist Priscilla Shirer said, "God does not speak to be heard. He speaks to be obeyed." If you want to chase purpose instead of money as you create your wealthy life, you must answer when you're called, not just when you feel good enough. Choose obedience over avoidance and excuses. Choose obedience over expectation, logic, and convenience. Choose obedience over perfection.

### Redefine Wealth for Yourself

Check yourself for areas of resistance. What part of your purpose have you been waiting to pursue until you can do it perfectly? Commit to taking action on it within the next week.

## 96. ALLOW PURPOSE TO EVOLVE

I first came across Tabitha Brown on Facebook before she became a social media star. At the time, I thought she was hilarious and engaging and made vegan food fun and sexy. She made viewers want to try dishes that would otherwise sound totally unappealing. Her purpose was to share her love of vegan food because switching to a plant-based diet helped her resolve health issues.

As of this writing, she has over 4 million followers on TikTok, and Tabitha, also an actress, has signed with one of the top talent agencies in Hollywood. Even if she had hopes of going viral when she shot her first video, there's no way she could have predicted her path. Most of us had never heard of TikTok, the platform where she has her largest following, but she allowed the method she used to fulfill her purpose to evolve, and it paid off for her in so many ways.

Tabitha may have had a vision for what she wanted to create, but if she had waited until she could see the whole picture, she would never have taken the first step. She'd still be shopping for the right lights, trying to figure out how to shoot the perfect video, and researching what makes a video go viral. Instead, she took advantage of new opportunities as they opened up for her.

As your purpose evolves, so should the rewards you receive for working in your purpose. Even if you've found your purpose in working for a nonprofit with low salary caps, it can evolve to create new opportunities for you to earn more without chasing money as a consultant If you're a middle manager, your purpose may evolve into climbing to new levels of leadership or launching your own business.

I'm cognizant of the systemic issues at play here. However, no matter what your gender or ethnicity might be, and regardless of the any oppression, you can't avoid your role in working in your purpose. If you're trying to evolve and conditions aren't favorable with your employer or in your town, you can always go somewhere else. If your company doesn't have room for growth, you have to either be okay with making the move to another company or admit you're sacrificing your purpose to stay where you're comfortable. You always have a choice.

Nothing you decide today has to be permanent. Don't hold yourself back. Be willing to do whatever it takes to do purposeful work. If the job you have now doesn't allow you to grow with your purpose, be willing to move on, leaving friends and familiarity behind. If the business you want to launch today might not be what you want to do for the rest of your life, launch it anyway and know that you can always change course when the time comes.

> **Redefine Wealth for Yourself**
> Are you working in your purpose now? Are you being fairly compensated for the value you provide? Are there ways you want to create more value and earn more money? Identify the next step in the evolution of your purpose and take action to make it happen.

## 97. NEGOTIATE WITH AUTHORITY

Growing up, I watched my mother work hard to get the best price on everything. There was no looking up prices online back then. Instead, she flipped through circulars and catalogs to compare prices. When she found a vacuum cleaner she wanted, she checked the Montgomery Ward and JCPenney catalogs to see which store had the better deal. (I understand if you have no idea what those stores are. I just aged myself considerably here.) By the time we got to Montgomery Ward, only one of the model she wanted was left on the floor.

Standing in the middle of the department store, my mother went back and forth with the clerk over the price. The more she haggled, the more embarrassed I felt. She was willing to go to war over a $16-dollar price difference, and I couldn't understand why, so I popped on my Walkman and wandered away, hoping no one would associate me with my mother. I decided I'd never be a haggler. I'd rather pay the asking price and not make a scene. As a Black woman, I didn't want to look poor or like I was trying to take advantage of anyone.

My resistance to haggling lasted into adulthood. Not long ago, my assistant informed me I hadn't used a subscription plan for months, so I told her to cancel it. She then asked me if she should also request that the company prorate our bill and refund some of the money. I told her I didn't have time for that, but if she wanted to do it, she should go ahead. She went back and forth with them over a couple of days, and in the end, they refunded $670—all because she was willing to negotiate. Her initiative and the results she got inspired me to rethink my stance on "haggling."

Haggling to save $16 on an appliance might not make a huge difference for you, but negotiating to get several hundred of your hard-earned dollars returned certainly can. More importantly, how you negotiate the salary and benefits for your job or a contract for your services can have a major impact on your financial wellbeing. A 2019 study found that while sixty-eight percent of men negotiated their salary, only forty-five percent of women did.[12] Perhaps some women don't realize negotiating is an option, but what seems like a dream job that allows you to do purposeful work can quickly become the job you hate when you feel like you're being underpaid for your value and your time.

Negotiating with authority is a skill you need to learn. If feelings of unworthiness or embarrassment stand in your way, go back to the FIT pillar and work on your mental fitness and your mindset. Do your research, get the facts and figures, and remove the emotion from the process so you can negotiate your way to earning more.

### Redefine Wealth for Yourself

Where can you negotiate to earn more? If you work a traditional job, research where your salary falls within your company, in your industry, and as compared to similar positions in other industries. Use this information when you request a raise, apply for a promotion, or look for a new job.

If you're an entrepreneur, assess the prices you charge for your products and services. Are your prices based on the value you provide, what your competitors charge, or something else? Do you need to negotiate higher prices on future deals?

# PART VI. MONEY

## Manage What You Have Wisely

I F YOU SKIPPED straight to this section because you want to work on MONEY pillar and deal with the rest later, stop here. This pillar is last for a reason. Your money is a byproduct of how much you invest in solidifying the first five pillars—FIT, PEOPLE, SPACE, FAITH, and WORK. Each of these directly impacts your results with money. At the same time, it does you no good to have a six-figure bank balance if your family is in shambles or you have no faith practices to rely upon when you have problems money can't solve. If you don't know how to rest when you need to, all the material wealth in the world can't help you. If you're developing high blood pressure because you go to a job you hate every day, the luxury SUV you drive to the office means nothing. Money is just one element of a wealthy life.

The basics of personal finance aren't complicated. Spend less than you make. Earn more. Save consistently. Minimize debt and take it on wisely. Invest in vehicles you understand. It really is as simple as that. However, it's hard to make those basics regular habits when the rest of your life isn't in order. The Six Pillars of Wealth are designed to guide you to create harmony and alignment in every area of your life, producing a sense of peace that frees you to manage your money. If you've worked through the first five pillars, you're ready to deal with money from a place of strength, confidence, and wellbeing.

**CHAPTER 16**

# Elevate Your Money Mindset

L IKE MOST PEOPLE, while I grew up with money messages all
around me, I received very few intentional lessons about how money
works or what's required to build lasting material wealth. However,
at eighteen years old, I took the initiative to learn a little more about
money on my own. I studied the basics of personal finance, but along the
way, I also picked up the idea that creating wealth was all about tactical
skills. So I learned how to budget, I saved the recommended percentage
of my income, and I opened all the right bank accounts. Once I built my
seven-figure business using those skills, I expected my net worth and
the rich lifestyle that came with it could only get better.

When my financial ascent came to an abrupt end with the Great
Recession, it caught me completely off guard. I couldn't understand
where I'd gone wrong. I believed if you got good grades, went to college
and earned more good grades, and did something productive with your
life, everything would be fine. I'd done all those things. Yet somehow,
I still wound up shaking out old purses and digging between couch
cushions to scrounge for change to put gas in the car. I'd been gener-
ous and fair with people, and I'd run my business with integrity, but
I ended up at the welfare office applying for food stamps to feed my
newborn daughter.

When I tell the story of how I started my career as America's Money Maven, I often paraphrase the verse that set me on my new course after I lost everything. *What good is money in the hands of a fool if they have no desire to seek wisdom?* Finding Proverbs 17:16 at my lowest point opened my eyes to where I'd gone astray. For so long, I believed education was the key to creating wealth. I studied hard. I got my real estate and mortgage broker's licenses at twenty-one years old, and I earned multiple certifications. I had so much knowledge, but very little wisdom.

All the education in the world will not save you if you don't have judgment and perspective to know how to apply the information you've consumed. Your money skill set can be deep and wide, but without an understanding of how money is attracted and repelled, as well as a belief system to support a wealthy life, you'll always find ways to self-sabotage. Like I did, and like so many people who desire a wealthy life, you'll end up right back where you started. Without wisdom, your money mindset will keep you stuck and you'll never be able to get ahead.

The results you've gotten with money up to this point are all a result of how you think about it. Your savings and investments, your monthly salary, and your debt all flow from your money mindset and whether it's grounded in wisdom or limiting beliefs. Elevate your money mindset, and you'll cease struggling to create and keep the wealth you want because, ultimately, wealth has a zero percent to do with money and one hundred percent to do with how you think about money.

## 98. WEALTH IS A CHOICE

On the second most downloaded episode of my podcast, I had the pleasure of interviewing Dr. Dennis Kimbro, educator and bestselling author of *Think and Grow Rich: A Black Choice*. During our conversation, Dr. Kimbro, who has served as my longtime mentor, shared a story about his lowest financial point. At the time, he was committed to writing and publishing his first book, but he had no money coming in. His home fell into foreclosure, and the two family cars were repossessed. Dr. Kimbro felt like a failure as a husband and a father.

One evening, in the middle of their financial crisis, his wife insisted they go out for dinner at a Chinese restaurant and have a moment's respite from the constant stress of making ends meet. However, instead of taking his mind off his problems for an hour or two, Dr. Kimbro spent the whole time bemoaning the state of his financial affairs. At the end of dinner, the server brought over fortune cookies, and Dr. Kimbro cracked one open, but he didn't like what he read. The fortune had nothing to do with his life or what he needed to hear, but rather than accept the fortune he was handed, he decided he had a choice. He went from table to table, picking up unopened fortune cookies left by other patrons until he found a fortune that worked for him. It read: "You will be surrounded by faith and funds." This was a message he could receive and hold on to.

Back at home, Dr. Kimbro invited his wife and daughters to join him in the living room, and standing in a circle, the family held hands as he told them, "Take a good look. This is the basement floor. You will never see this again in life." He promised his family they'd only go up from there. He went to work on his book, finished it, and sent it out. Two months after that dinner, twelve of the top publishing houses went into a bidding war for his book, which sold for the kind of advance most authors only dream of earning.

As he watched his financial situation become more critical, Dr. Kimbro made a choice. He could have accepted the fortune life gave him, but he chose to seek the fortune he deserved. He could have given up when things got hard, but he chose to honor his purpose and persevere. He pushed to finish, sell, and publish his book, and his efforts were rewarded.

Like Dr. Kimbro, you always have a choice. You never have to just accept whatever life gives you. Instead, you can keep reaching for a new fortune cookie. You can choose to launch your first business, find new clients, or pivot to a new industry. You can decide to develop new skills and seek work with better compensation. You can choose not to take unsolicited advice or let anyone interfere with your plans. Make decisions in alignment with your purpose and core values and choose to create a life of material wealth without ever chasing money.

> ### *Redefine Wealth for Yourself*
> You always have a choice to take wealth-building action or not.
> Make a list of the areas in your life where you need to make a
> new choice to create the material wealth you want. Decide to
> choose wealth, in all its forms, from this day forward.

## 99. REWRITE YOUR FINANCIAL BLUEPRINT

In a Mastery + Momentum mastermind session, I encouraged the women
to assess their growth in the first five pillars—FIT, PEOPLE, SPACE,
FAITH, and, WORK—and identify any connections between that growth
and changes in their financial situation. One woman talked about how
her faith had improved dramatically during her time in our mastermind
group. She was surprised to discover how little she'd trusted God before
joining the program and had chosen to intentionally develop her faith.

Putting her faith in God freed her from constant worry about her
finances. She went from afraid to open her bills to a place of peace. In
the process of growing her faith, she released her scarcity mindset. As
she obeyed God more, she received an unexpected windfall she received
an unexpected windfall, and used it to pay off all her debt. Diving into
the Bible and God's promises led her to trust God more, which inspired
her to rewrite her financial blueprint, choose new beliefs about money
and how it works, and make better financial decisions.

Like everyone else, you have a set of beliefs about money, what it means
when you have plenty of it, and what it means when you find yourself in a
state of lack. You have thoughts about how much is enough, how much is
too much, what people should or should not do to get money, and what
it says about you if you desire money. Most of these beliefs you learned
early in life from your parents, teachers, religious leaders, and the media.

Observing how the adults in your life handled a layoff, a bankruptcy,
or a surplus of money and hearing how they communicated about money
matters informed your financial blueprint. If your parents said things
like "Money doesn't grow on trees," "It takes money to make money," or

"Black women have to work twice as hard to earn half as much," you likely internalized those beliefs. Finding eviction notices on the front door, coming home to a dark house because someone failed to pay the electric bill, watching celebrities live lavish lifestyles you couldn't afford, or at the opposite extreme, always having enough money to do and have whatever you wanted—these experiences shaped the way you think about money.

The financial blueprint you developed throughout childhood and adolescence may well be causing you to sabotage your success with money today. If you're not achieving your money goals, examine the primary influences that shaped the way you think about money. Your money blueprint isn't written in stone. Just like you can learn a new language or how to draw in adulthood, you can learn to elevate your money mindset. Design a new money blueprint for yourself, one that creates a mindset of abundance and keeps you focused on the reality that all your money goals are possible for you.

### Redefine Wealth for Yourself

Make a list of all the money influences you can think of from your childhood, including sayings, events, or habits you observed or experienced. Next to each one, write how it has impacted your current financial life. If the influence is positive, great. Keep that element of your financial blueprint. If not, write exactly how you'll replace it with thoughts and beliefs that serve your money goals.

## 100. AFFIRM YOURSELF TO WEALTH

In 2018, on a special question-and-answer episode of the podcast, a listener wrote in to ask, "What helped you believe you were worth the accolades, the money, the opportunities, and the titles?" The answer was easy. I didn't always believe it. I wasn't always clear about my worth. I had to work to recognize the value of what I contributed to the world, and affirmations were essential to that process.

When I was recovering from losing my business, I knew if I sought wisdom, I'd be better than okay. However, in the beginning, I didn't have a clear game plan. I first needed to figure out how to believe I was more than my losses, mistakes, and failures. To do that, I honed in on my gift and acknowledged that God had called me to do something valuable. I had experienced a set of circumstances—losing my money—but those circumstances were not me. They didn't define my worth.

It took some time, but the power of affirmations helped me grow in this area. Every day, I said to myself, "I deserve to be wealthy because of the value I add to others." As I took on this belief, I committed to pouring into other people. Anyone who makes a significant contribution, in any field, deserves to be wealthy. People who are willing to stand up, stand out, and take the risk, face the ridicule, and deal with the rejection, deserve the resulting accolades, money, opportunities, and titles. Affirmations helped me solidify my belief in the value I was creating, which led me to give more, and thus, I received more.

Earlier, I described how you can use affirmations to change the way you think about yourself and to take responsibility for the results you create in your life. Wealth affirmations will help you practice believing thoughts that make it possible for you to create material wealth. They'll support you in replacing any limiting beliefs you have about money with thoughts that serve you in achieving your money goals.

Here are some of the wealth affirmations I've shared with my community:

- *Financial abundance is my birthright.*
- *My financial cup is overflowing.*
- *I am the master of my wealth.*
- *My gifts constantly place me in the presence of greatness.*
- *My work is valued and appreciated in the world.*

Those affirmations have worked for me, but the most effective affirmations are the ones you create for yourself. Challenge the old beliefs that have shackled you with debt, caused you to settle for being underpaid, or otherwise made you fall short of your wealth goals. Create your own affirmations to replace those limiting beliefs.

Follow the examples below to rewrite your limiting beliefs about money.

- **Old belief:** I never have enough money.
- **Wealth affirmation:** *Wealth constantly flows into my life.*

- **Old belief:** Money is the root of all evil.
- **Wealth affirmation:** *I use money to better my life and the lives of others.*

- **Old belief:** I don't know how to make money.
- **Wealth affirmation:** *I create a new stream of income every year.*

Move past the thinking that has kept you stuck in your finances and take on a fresh perspective. You get to decide what you think about wealth and your ability to have more material resources in your life. Choose to affirm your way to wealth.

## Redefine Wealth for Yourself

Choose three to five wealth affirmations you want to take on as beliefs. Write them on sticky notes and post them where you'll read them every day. Say them out loud to yourself several times a day until you begin to recognize them as truth. Take one small action each week to lead you in the direction of what you've committed to affirm. Then, start the process over with new wealth affirmations.

# 101. ADD VISUALS TO YOUR MONEY GOALS

My client Shante had a makeup problem. When she found me through an article in *Upscale* magazine, she was a self-confessed beauty junkie. Rather than save for her big money goals, she overspent at Sephora every month. When we talked, I suggested Shante keep her goals where she could see them and add a visual representation of what she wanted to achieve. She'd always wanted to move to France before she settled down to have a family, so she wrote "I live in Paris" on the front of her debit card and taped a picture of the Eiffel Tower on the back.

Whenever Shante took out her card to make a purchase, she was reminded of her big goal. Every time she saw the Eiffel Tower, she had to ask herself if another lipstick or eye shadow was worth more to her than her dream. In the following months, she stopped spending on beauty products she didn't need and started saving. Those small decisions quickly added up, and eventually, she saved enough money to quit her job in New York and make the move to Paris, where she lived for several months.

When you set goals, your brain connects more to images than to words. Vague words like "travel," "house," or "new car" don't create the emotional connection necessary to keep you motivated over the long haul. An image of something you deeply care about can serve as a concrete reminder of what's important to you. You can use vision boards, but you won't always have your vision board in front of you. Find images that keep your money goals top of mind in the moments when you make spending decisions and keep those images nearby.

### Redefine Wealth for Yourself

Choose images to represent your most important money goals—something that represents the country you want to visit, the business you want to launch, the baby you want to have, or the vacation you want to take. Put the images where you'll see them when you make money decisions. Your wallet, debit card, and phone screensaver are great places to start. Let those visuals guide the decisions you make for saving and spending your money.

# 102. PICK UP PENNIES

When I was a freshman at the University of Southern California, a student in his junior year spoke to the Black students in our class. DeVon Franklin wasn't yet a best-selling author, TV and film producer, or spiritual success coach as he is today, but he had some words of wisdom for us. When we entered the room, there was a twenty-dollar bill on the floor in front of the stage, and DeVon asked, "Who wants to pick that up?" We all kept our seats, not wanting to fall for a trick, not wanting to look dumb. Finally, a young lady picked up the money and went back to her seat.

DeVon made the point that money and opportunities are always all around us but most of us will either never notice them or never have the guts to take advantage of them. We're too busy, too worried about what other people will think, or too cynical and suspicious. That day, I let the other student beat me to the money, but I decided I would never walk over an opportunity again.

After that, it seemed I spotted loose change everywhere I went, and when I did, I grabbed it. I was always picking up pennies on campus. My friends laughed, but I didn't care. Soon, I found five-dollar and ten-dollar bills. I observed people leaving their change after transactions and young people tossing pennies in the street like they were skipping stones across a pond, and I shook my head in disbelief as I picked up the coins. Didn't they know, I wondered, that they were disrespecting money and throwing away opportunities?

I was all in with picking up pennies until I reached a certain level of success. I imagined people would look at me funny if I stepped out of a Land Rover and picked up a quarter in the parking lot. However, I challenged that thought. Those same people would certainly stop to pick up a hundred-dollar bill. It's not about the amount of money that matters. Collecting change was my way of showing respect for the money placed right there in my path.

Not long ago, I was at LAX, and on the way to my gate, I noticed so much change on the floor. I was dressed to the nines, wheeling designer luggage, and headed to the first-class line. I hesitated to pick up the change, but I reminded myself of how many opportunities we miss when we think we're too good to reach out and take them. I picked up that change and held my head up as I boarded with the rest of first class. I'm sure other people had seen the money on the ground, but they either didn't value it or didn't value it more than they cared about the opinions of a bunch of strangers who might judge them for bending over to pick up coins. It was their loss.

I'm a money magnet. I attract money, and when I do, I respect it and accept it. You can be a money magnet too. All you have to do is open your eyes to the pennies and dollar bills all around you, just waiting for someone to pick them up. Respect money enough to bend down and get it when it offers itself to you. Respect opportunity enough to seize it when it flings itself at your feet.

### Redefine Wealth for Yourself

The next time you're in a drive-through, open your door, lean down, and pick up the change lying there on the asphalt. Trust me; there's usually plenty there for the taking. As you go through self-checkout at the grocery store, pick up the pennies someone else saw as worthless and tossed aside. Get in the habit of seeing and receiving money—and opportunities—everywhere you go.

## 103. EXPECT SURPRISE CHECKS

When I lived in Metairie, Louisiana, at my financial low point, much of my mail went to my mother's house in Los Angeles. After it piled up a bit, she stuck it all in a manila envelope and sent it to me. However, when I received it, I didn't open it. I figured it was all bills and notices from debt collectors, and I didn't want to deal with it. Over the following weeks, I forgot all about the envelope.

Several months later, I stumbled across the mail my mother had forwarded to me. This time, I took a deep breath and decided to deal with it. Inside I found plenty of bills, as I'd expected, but I also found a check for $300, a refund for an overpayment I'd made on a bill. Unfortunately, the check had expired a few weeks after I received it.

A few hundred dollars would have been a huge blessing for my family and me, but instead of cashing the check and buying diapers and food, I'd let it sit there until it became a worthless piece of paper. Avoiding my mail didn't change my situation for the better. In fact, expecting the worst had cost me some of the relief I'd been hoping and praying to get. After that, I trained myself to greet my mail with a smile, open everything, and expect surprise checks. I became more aware of my financial situation, and sometimes, those surprise checks showed up. I've gotten unexpected insurance payments, payouts from class action lawsuits I'd forgotten I was a part of, and almost $1000 from an old inactive bank account.

A few weeks after I shared this story at one of the Paul Mitchell Schools, a student sent me a message. She'd gone through her mail with excitement and expectation for the first time in a long time, and her surprise check had arrived. Unexpectedly, she received a check for $2000 from a class action lawsuit. In her old mindset, she would've either missed it altogether or thought it was a scam and tossed it, but because she expected it, she wasn't thrown. She verified that it was real, and deposited the much-needed funds in her account.

Those pieces of paper in your mailbox aren't just mail. They represent the movement of your money as it flows toward you and away from you. Your mail can bring you bills and debt collection, but it can also bring you financial relief. Start expecting surprise checks and watch how many show up for you.

### Redefine Wealth for Yourself

Make it a habit to regularly collect, sort, and read your mail, and do it with excitement and anticipation. Face the bills and debts with a positive attitude and stay ready for surprise checks among the envelopes.

## CHAPTER 17

# Master the Basics

O N A MASTERY + Momentum group coaching call, one of our members shared that prior to joining the mastermind, she believed she had a lot to learn about money. However, as she developed more confidence, she realized she already knew a lot about money. She just needed to take action. She started consistently applying the basic money principles she already knew. She stopped wasting money on things she didn't need and paid off debt. She stopped worrying about which savings account was the best, chose a percentage of her salary to save every month, and started saving. Without learning anything new or hiring a financial advisor, she increased her wealth.

The fundamentals of money management aren't complicated. It's a safe bet you already know you should stop adding to your credit card debt and pay it off. You're well aware that you should save a portion of your salary every month. The common-sense advice you've heard from your parents and grandparents, from money experts on talk shows, and from personal finance books doesn't change. However, if you've done the work in the first five pillars, you'll be able to see old information through a new lens of holistic wealth as you look at the principles in this chapter. You'll be in a much better space to receive and implement the information. Elevate your financial status to the next level of wealth by mastering the basics.

## 104. PINPOINT THE VOID

I have an acquaintance who buys a new car every year. He makes the purchase with a lot of fanfare, so no one in his life can miss the fact that he has a new ride. His car payment and loan balance increase year after year as he rolls one loan into the next. At one point, he had a $1700 monthly payment for a Range Rover. That's more than the median monthly mortgage payment in this country, which is around $1500.[13] This type of self-destructive spending behavior is almost always an attempt to fill a void, to replace something else that's missing in the person's life.

Psychologist and behavioral finance expert Dr. Daniel Crosby, PhD, describes how insecurities about his background led him to purchase a huge house that came with unexpected problems and expenses and failed to make him happy in the way he expected. The son of a financial advisor, Dr. Crosby wrote *The Laws of Wealth* and *The Behavioral Investor*. He's an expert on behavioral finance, but that doesn't make him exempt from some of the pitfalls of human behavior when it comes to money.

Overspending, bad investments, and other financial mismanagement are often symptoms of a lack fulfillment or a desire to fill a void. When something fundamental is missing in their life, many people will buy more stuff and experiences or attempt to pay for attention and affection from other people to try fill the hole. As they inevitably discover, money can buy security and opportunity, but it can't buy happiness. Filling your closet with more shoes, buying a new car every year, running up credit card debt to stay at a resort you can't afford, or paying bills for adult children or loved ones who are perfectly capable of supporting themselves—these are all efforts to fill a void. While they may make you feel better for a moment, the high never lasts.

Once you pinpoint the void, figure out why you're making these choices, and do the work to heal, you can successfully follow through with your money basics. In hindsight, Dr. Crosby suggests he would've been better served going to therapy before making such a significant purchase because the house he was so enamored with when he first walked through it is now just another house. It's nice, but it's not life-changing. Like Dr. Crosby, we all have times when we want to feel better and mistakenly think buying something new will solve the problem. However, healing the void goes back to the FIT pillar. Taking care of your mental health will help you manage the voids in a healthy way. Then, you can make financial decisions based on your budget and your financial goals, not out of a desire to feel loved, important, or respected.

> **Redefine Wealth for Yourself**
> Get honest with yourself about the financial missteps you've made in the past. Dig deep and figure out what void you may have been trying to fill. Talk with a psychologist skilled in this area to figure out how to fill the void in a healthy manner and avoid making similar unproductive choices in the future. For support from a skilled professional with expertise in this area, visit financialtherapyassociation.org to locate a financial therapist in your area.

## 105. FIND THE MISSING MONEY

A 2018 study by the Federal Reserve found that four in ten Americans would struggle to cover an unexpected $400 expense in any given month.[14] For many people, this comes down to a need to earn more income. They barely make enough to pay their bills each month, so an unanticipated expense can send them scrambling to use credit cards, borrow from a relative or friend, or turn to lenders that may be predatory in their practices. However, many of the people I talk to earn more than enough to make ends meet and still struggle to handle unanticipated expenses.

A fundamental element of redefining wealth for yourself is having a vision for every part your life, including your money. Your budget is your vision for your money. This simple document records how and when your money will come in and outlines how it should go out, so you're not stuck trying to run tallies in your head or guessing whether or not you'll have enough money to make it to the end of the month. Thinking through your budget can also prevent unexpected expenses because you can plan in advance for things most people treat like an emergency, like new tires for your car, air conditioner repair, and replacing outdated or broken technology.

Your budget is also an essential tool for identifying any holes in your financial planning. If you want to save more, invest, or pay off debt, but can't seem to figure out how you can possibly do it all, a budget will help you find the missing money. Your budget sets the tone for your financial plan and provides the foundation for developing wealthy habits as you increase your discipline in this area.

As the CEO of your life, you have the opportunity to make financial decisions based on facts. Your budget will make it easy for you to see the facts of how much money you have, the debt you own, how much you've saved, and what you're investing. It will help you identify where you can find the money you need to accomplish unmet goals. Run your household finances like a business, making decisions based on the numbers, not on emotions.

### Redefine Wealth for Yourself

Create a monthly budget for your household. Include all income sources and list all expenses. Decide in advance how much you'll spend on variable categories, like food and clothing, and discretionary expenses, like dining out and entertainment. Use your budget to make spending decisions throughout the month, and if you need to spend more than planned in one category, make sure you take that money from another category.

## 106. BUY BACK YOUR FREEDOM

I met Jason Vitug on the dance floor at FinCon, a conference for personal finance educators and content creators. At the time, we talked about our forthcoming books, my second and his first. We both went home and made those books happen, and because of our last names, our books are often next to each other on the bookstore shelves. Jason wrote *You Only Live Once* to help people achieve their best life through mindful money practices.

Jason went from living paycheck to paycheck, even while he earned a six-figure salary, to paying off his debt and stacking up significant savings. He quit his six-figure job with a financial institution to backpack round the world, traveling to twenty countries over twelve months. Through his experience, he came up with the concept of a freedom fund. Jason encourages people to escape the trap of working fifty weeks a year just to have two weeks of vacation, often at jobs they don't love. He suggests you create a freedom fund and save to buy back your freedom.

Jason tells people to look at the cost of any discretionary purchase not just in terms of dollars but also in terms of the hours they'll have to work to pay for any one item. For example, if you make $20 an hour, and you pay $500 for a plasma TV, you'll spend 25 work hours on that TV. Look at those numbers and decide if the TV is worth the work or if you'd rather invest that work and the resulting income in something that will get you closer to freedom, however you define it. The TV might be worth it to you because you and your spouse love movies and will get years of entertainment value from it. Or you might decide you'd rather invest those work hours in your dream house, your trip to Cuba, or to enroll in a course that will help you launch your business. In those moments, you can decide to buy things or buy freedom. The choice is yours.

Many people think of YOLO as permission to buy the TV, splurge on the shoes, or treat all their friends to dinner. But Jason teaches that if you only live once, you probably don't want to spend that life working to pay for frivolous things. Get clear about what you're working for and invest in buying back your freedom.

### Redefine Wealth for Yourself

Take a moment to calculate your hourly wage, factoring in the number of hours you actually work in a week, and the number of weeks you work per year.

Note the difference in the example below:

$75,000 ÷ 40 hours/week ÷ 50 weeks (with 2 weeks' vacation) = $37.50/hour

$75,000 ÷ 60 hours/week ÷ 50 (with 2 weeks' vacation) = $25/hour

Whenever you want to make a discretionary purchase, calculate the number of hours you'll have to work to pay for it, and decide whether you'll spend that money or save it to invest in your freedom.

## 107. EXECUTE YOUR DEBT ELIMINATOR

A 2019 Consumer Debt Study, conducted by Experian, found the average American carried $90,460 in debt with average credit card balances of over $6000.[15] Most debt is expensive. Not only do you have to spend some of your monthly income on payments, but you also pay interest, and should you fall behind, penalties and fees. Eliminate your debt and you rid yourself of that burden and free yourself to spend that money in ways that serve you better.

Financial experts all have their favorite system for getting rid of debt. I call my system the debt eliminator, and I consider it a first cousin to the debt-snowball method made popular by money expert Dave Ramsey. One of the benefits of the debt eliminator is the ability to pinpoint a date when your debt will be paid in full so you can work toward your freedom date.

Here's how the debt eliminator system works:

**Step 1.** Create a realistic budget and determine how much you can apply to your debt eliminator each month. This may require you to work extra hours, close more sales, or cut discretionary spending in the short term.

**Step 2.** Determine your debt eliminator: the amount you'll apply to debt above the monthly minimum payments. How much money in your current budget can be redirected towards the smallest debt?

**Step 3.** List all debts in ascending order, from the smallest balance to the largest. Alternatively, you can prioritize your debts in the order of the highest interest rate or by greatest amount owed. However, I suggest you work smallest to largest. This method allows you to pay off the first debt much faster. The satisfaction of that accomplishment will keep you motivated and on track with the remaining debts. If two debts are very close in balance, then target the debt with the higher interest rate to pay off first.

**Step 4.** Pay your debt eliminator on that smallest debt until it's paid off. Some lenders, like mortgage lenders and car companies, will automatically apply extra amounts towards the next payment, so contact your lenders in advance and request the extra payments go directly toward principal reduction. They'll likely tell you the best way to make sure that happens is to indicate your preference with each payment. If so, make that call every month. Credit card companies don't typically need this instruction. The entire payment will go toward the current balance.

**Step 5.** Continue to pay the minimum payment on all other debts.

**Step 6.** Once you pay the first debt in full, add your full debt eliminator amount to the minimum payment of the next smallest balance. This new sum becomes your new debt eliminator and the monthly payment for the second smallest debt.

**Step 7.** Repeat until all debts are paid in full.

Work out the numbers for each of these steps on paper first, using debt eliminator amounts and monthly payments to calculate when each debt will be paid in full. For simple numbers, divide the balance of the smallest debt by the debt eliminator. This will tell you approximately how many months it should take to pay off that debt.

If the first debt will take six months to pay off, subtract six months of minimum payments from your other debts. Then, apply the new debt eliminator to the next debt, working out the numbers to find out how many months it will take to pay off all your debts.

It's important to note the debt eliminator doesn't suggest you look for extra money to pay your debts because it's almost impossible for most of us to find "extra" money in our budgets. However, when you're intentional about your budget bringing in extra income, and cutting back on discretionary spending, you can apply that money to reducing and eliminating your debt.

### Redefine Wealth for Yourself

If you're carrying debt, create your debt eliminator and commit to seeing it through to the end. For additional support, use a visual debt elimination tracker. I love the Debt Free Charts by Michael Lacy at winningtowealth.com/shop. They allow you to color in your progress as you pay down credit cards, medical bills, mortgage debt, car loans, and more.

## 108. CREATE AN OPPORTUNITY FUND

I was getting miked and ready to go on the air when the morning news host asked me about the opportunity fund I teach about in *Real Money Answers for Every Woman*, the book I was there to promote. I explained that I believed we should save for opportunities instead of emergencies because we're more likely to save for what we want than we are to save for a vague idea of something that might, or might not, happen in the future. When she responded that she'd always believed in emergency funds, I said, "In my experience, most people just aren't inspired by that."

She looked at me and said, "You're wrong, and I think you're leading people astray." Seconds later, she introduced me to her audience. "We're live with America's Money Maven."

Maybe she was a numbers woman, someone highly motivated by watching the balance in her bank account grow. Maybe her desire to avoid risk far outweighed her impulse to buy something she might enjoy. I never got the chance to discuss it with her further, but if I had, I would've explained that the average person doesn't think that way. In the interviews that followed, I drilled down on the opportunity fund and really drove it home because I knew there were naysayers like her who would try to dissuade people from using this money strategy.

As humans, we're built to survive today. Most people don't have the mental bandwidth to think about the long term. Getting the average person to focus on a problem that could potentially happen months or years down the road, when they're faced with the needs and desires of today, is heavy lifting. It's a lot more appealing to save for the vacation they've dreamed of taking, the conference they want to attend, or the new business venture they want to launch. Scaring people into saving is tough because most people don't want to think about what could go wrong somewhere down the road.

I prefer to focus on what I want to magnify and bring forth, so I don't put words like "rainy day" and "emergency" next to my money. It's important to save even as you pay down debt because your opportunity fund can prevent you from taking on additional debt in the future. Of course, emergencies will still arise, but when you've created a solid opportunity fund, you have the opportunity to transform what would've been a crisis into a mere inconvenience.

### Redefine Wealth for Yourself

It's important to save, even as you pay down debt, because your opportunity fund can prevent you from taking on additional debt in the future. Make saving a regular line item in your budget and set milestones you'll hit by saving a consistent percentage of your income. Focus on the opportunities you'll take advantage of with the money you've set aside.

## 109. KNOW YOUR NUMBERS

When I provided financial counseling through a nonprofit organization, I observed many habits that kept people in poverty or living below the standard they desired. One of the biggest issues was a lack of knowledge about their own money. Most people just didn't know their numbers.

Whenever a new client came in, I started with the basics, going over the reality of their income and expenses. Without fail, whenever I asked about rent or mortgage, they answered easily. However, as we moved on to other expenses, like utilities and groceries, they'd look up as if their monthly budget was written in the air. I'd lean to the side and look at the ceiling too and ask, "Did someone tape your gas bill up there?" We'd laugh, but most people couldn't tell me what they spent on clothing, electricity, gas, or auto expenses in a typical month. They just didn't know.

Not only did they not know how much they were spending, but some of these people assumed they had bad credit scores because they'd had bad debt at some point in life. When we checked their score and it was above average, they were shocked. They had passed on home ownership programs or jobs that required a credit check because they assumed they wouldn't qualify. More than one client cried in my office when they realized they could've applied for and gotten a better job and started earning more money months earlier. One man, a widower and single dad, explained he could've applied for a promotion at his current job, but he hadn't bothered because he'd been sure he had bad credit.

While my clientele at the nonprofit tended to have lower incomes, earning more doesn't necessarily equate to being savvier about your finances. Many people earn a good living and still can't tell you where much of their money goes. They, like my former clients, assume the worst and avoid digging into the numbers because what they find might require them to change. None of this is healthy money management. If you don't know where you're starting, it's impossible to create a plan for where you're going or to determine how long it will take you to get there.

Make it a point to know the ins and outs of your income and expenses. Keep track of your credit score and what appears on your credit report. Know your numbers so you can make financial decisions from a place of awareness and wisdom, rather than from a place of ignorance or fear.

*Redefine Wealth for Yourself*
If you haven't pulled your credit report in the last six months, do it today. Check your credit score and review the report for any errors or surprises. Create a simple spreadsheet or sign-up for a personal finance app to track your income and expenses and schedule a time to review the numbers at least once a month.

## 110. GIVE CHEERFULLY

When I met the woman who would give me my start in real estate, I was a nineteen-year-old college student. Early in our relationship, I noticed that she gave a lot to people. Everyone around her noticed because she was always vocal about being a giver, who she gave to, and the amount she gave. Her giving always came with a story, often about what the recipient did or didn't do to show their gratitude. It quickly became obvious anything she gave came with strings attached. When it was time for us to part ways, she made sure to remind me of every single thing she'd done for me. She had done some things for me, but that kind of giving reeks of a scarcity mindset.

In 2016, more than a decade later, I was attending the Neighborhood Awards in Las Vegas when I received a long text message from the same woman. She had called me several times, and I'd chosen not to answer her calls since our relationship had long since ended. In the text message, she enumerated the many things she'd given me or done for me in the past. "If it wasn't for me, you would never have known about real estate," she complained. Clearly, her mindset hadn't evolved since we last talked.

Giving is a fundamental wealth habit, but only when you give from a place of generosity. Sharing your wealth, or even your knowledge and wisdom, because you expect something in return is a form of manipulation. Being a cheerful giver requires you to give without expecting to receive anything in return. When you believe in abundance, you have an awareness that your giving spirit will be reciprocated beyond what you can imagine. You may never receive anything from the person or organization you gave to, but you know everything you put out will come back multiplied.

Healthy giving doesn't come from a place of expectation, and it isn't born out of guilt. If you give so other people won't be upset with you or disappointed, you're likely to end up disappointed in or upset with yourself. Give when it's the right thing *for you* to do. Give only when you can give with the best intentions and release your money with positivity attached to it.

### Redefine Wealth for Yourself

Take a moment to think about the last several times you gave. If you can't think of any occasions, then assess why you're holding so tightly to your money and where and with whom you might like to share your material wealth. If you can list several examples, consider why you gave each time and how the experience made you feel. Decide where and to whom you might like to give in the future.

## CHAPTER 18

# Introduce the Money Maven in You

EVERYONE, INCLUDING YOU, has a money maven somewhere inside them. Often, my clients tell me they're "not a money person," because they're creatives, authors, and speakers, but anyone can be a money person with a little effort. You have the ability to learn more about money and create material wealth for yourself. You can buckle down and do the work to change the trajectory of your finances. Master the basics, and then take your money knowledge and wisdom further. Dive deep into the money subjects that appeal to you. Seek wisdom and find wealth.

As you step into your identity as the money maven in your own life and your assets grow, you'll face new responsibilities. Not the least of these is your responsibility to own how money impacts your relationships. From the cousin who always needs a "loan" to the legacy you leave for the next generation, you're empowered to take control. The wisdom to handle these situations in the ways that best serve you and the people you care about will free you to achieve levels of wealth few people reach.

## 111. RECOGNIZE FINANCIAL ABUSE

When I worked in real estate, I didn't know the term "financial abuse," but I saw it happen all the time, most notably to grandparents who had worked a lifetime to pay off their homes. A grandchild would have no qualms about asking, manipulating, or coercing the grandparents to take out a line of credit against their house to finance the grandchild's business ventures. When the business fell apart—if it ever launched at all—the loan went unpaid, and the grandparents lost their home. From a buyer's standpoint, those were some of the best deals to be had, but the circumstances of the foreclosures were heartbreaking. The senior citizens who lost their homes struggled to find a decent place to live in what had become one of the most expensive cities in the country.

The elderly weren't the only ones suffering financial abuse at the hands of the people closest to them. In many cases, one spouse controlled all the finances, often under the guise of providing and protecting. The controlling spouse was usually, but not always, the husband. Even if he shared financial information with his wife, he manipulated the numbers so she had no idea what assets they owned or how much debt they were on the hook for as a couple. The wife went along thinking they were doing well until something unexpected happened, like her husband's untimely death or a need to borrow money. Then she discovered just how misled she'd been.

In other situations, one spouse, often but not always the wife, hid purchases. She left shopping bags in the trunk of her car and brought them in when her husband wasn't home. Some went so far as to leave new clothing purchases at a friend's house until they could rotate them into their wardrobe and pretend they'd had them for ages. Men, on the other hand, often hid the true cost of major purchases. In the most extreme cases, people bought secret investment properties, or they secretly spent their children's college funds. All this dishonesty around money amounted to financial infidelity, a form of financial abuse.

I understood there was something wrong in each of these instances, but not until years later did I come across the concept of financial abuse.

When I spoke with licensed clinical social worker and bestselling author of *Exposing Financial Abuse*, Shannon Thomas, on the podcast, she said money is often wielded as a weapon in relationships. She describes financial abuse as, "the hidden exploitation and control of finances." It includes anything from a person pressuring and manipulating friends or family members to take care of her financial needs to someone closing a victim's accounts and taking away any access she has to money. It includes the spouse or partner who claims they want to work and contribute, but always has an excuse why they can't, and church leadership demanding you give to the church first even when it means you can't provide for your family's basic needs.

If any of the above scenarios hits home for you, recognize that you may be involved in financial abuse. If you're the perpetrator, get honest with your spouse or whomever you're taking advantage of, and stop the behavior. If you struggle to stop on your own, or you believe your poor choices are tied to deeper issues, seek help from a psychologist or other licensed professional with experience in the area of financial abuse.

If you believe you have suffered or are currently experiencing financial abuse from someone in your life, you can put a stop to it. Decide to set boundaries, which may include removing yourself from the relationship. A qualified professional can help you decide what steps to take to move forward, so don't let shame or embarrassment prevent you from seeking help. Left unchecked, financial abuse can destroy relationships and traumatize the survivors. It will almost certainly keep you from living out your destiny and creating a wealthy life.

### Redefine Wealth for Yourself

Examine the role money plays in your relationships. If you see any hint of financial abuse, dig deeper. Make immediate changes where you can. If you need help, read *Exposing Financial Abuse*, and find a qualified mental health professional to help you set boundaries and deal with any trauma.

## 112. SAY "I'M SORRY I"

If you're used to being the person who comes to the financial rescue for your adult children, your best friend, your siblings, or other people in your life, changing that dynamic can feel difficult. Especially when you have the means, it's easy to want to be the savior. However, sometimes the best thing you can do to help friends and family who come to you for financial assistance is to decline to help. Saying no allows you to go from enabling their financial dependence to offering them the chance to mature and acknowledge they have agency to determine their own financial wellbeing. It's up to them to take it.

Many people struggle to say no to money requests. They'd rather lose hundreds or thousands of dollars than face potential conflict or rejection. This becomes easier when you keep in mind that you actually handicap people when you allow them to take advantage of you. You damage the relationship when you loan money you can't afford to give away or loan money to people who only need it because they refuse to learn to manage what they have.

In Chapter 4, "Protect Personal Relationships," I shared how you can set strong boundaries in your relationships. This is particularly important around the topic of money. Saying no and setting boundaries around your money is easier when you take accountability for your part in making the other person dependent on you. Set boundaries by starting the conversation with "I'm sorry I." When you try to change the relationship, people will object. They'll say things like: "But we've always done it this way," "You always let me do it in the past," and "You never said anything before." Preempting their objections with "I'm sorry, I" acknowledges up front that you have been a part of the problem.

Forgive yourself for the role you've played. Take a stand now and move forward. Statements like "I'm sorry I led you to believe I would continue to give you money" or "I'm sorry I made it seem like that was okay," you take away that person's argument that you're the one who set things up this way. Yes, you did allow the relationship to take a wrong turn. And now you're changing it for the better.

> ### *Redefine Wealth for Yourself*
> Prepare and practice for any "I'm sorry I" conversation you need to have in your life. Role play with a friend, so you can be ready for any objections. Use the script below, substituting details that apply, and be willing to stand behind the financial boundaries you set.
>
> *I'm sorry I led you to believe it was okay to borrow money from me and not return it. This actually made me feel really used at times. It wasn't right for me or for you. Going forward, if I choose to lend you money, it will be no more than $100, and we'll have a written contract with specific repayment arrangements.*

## 113. ONE-TIME GIFT

Occasionally, a relative reached out to me for help with her rent or the private school tuition for her children. At the time, my business was doing well, and from what I could see, I was financially better off than many members of my family so I wanted to help her. However, it soon became obvious that not having enough money to get through the month was a regular occurrence in her life. Rent is due on the same day every month, and tuition is paid on an agreed-upon schedule, so she knew she about these financial obligations and had the opportunity to plan for them or make other arrangements. Her poor planning wasn't a line item in my budget, and I didn't want it to become one.

Often, the best thing you can do to help someone is not to help, and I chose to stop giving my relative money. I didn't like feeling obligated or taken advantage of, and I hoped no longer serving as her safety net would motivate her to figure out how to improve her financial situation. The next time she asked, I used the "I'm sorry I" script to tell her I was sorry I'd led her to believe she could keep coming to me for money and I would no longer be able to offer her financial support.

Rather than leave her completely on her own, I added that, while I couldn't give her what she asked for, I could give her a smaller amount that worked for me *as a one-time gift*. Stressing that this was a one-time gift was important. I didn't want her to think we were in a negotiation or that she could always come back and get some amount of money from me. For her benefit and mine, I wanted to be clear that my financial support ended with that one check.

Many times, you'll simply say no to a request for money, as is your right. However, when you want to help to the extent that's comfortable for you, offer a one-time gift. Respond to the request with something like: "I'm sorry I can't solve that problem completely for you. But what I'd like to give you is a one-time gift in the amount of $X dollars. It's a gift, so you don't have to worry about paying it back, and we don't even have to talk about it again." When you send the money via check or payment app, write in the memo line "One-time gift." Then, stick to that declaration. Most people will get the message, and for those who don't, you can reference the initial conversation and move on.

### Redefine Wealth for Yourself

If you have friends or family who have constantly ask you for money, plan to offer them a one-time gift in lieu of ongoing support. Decide who this might apply to and rehearse what you'll say so you can say it with confidence when the time comes.

## 114. CHANGE THE NARRATIVE FOR THE NEXT GENERATION

At thirteen years old, my daughter Reagan sees very few limits. She's confident in ways I wasn't at her age. She doesn't know much yet about investing, but she knows she's an investor. She knows she's an owner. She knows she has the ability to create wealth for herself. Because her father and I have rewritten the narratives we grew up with, she sees her possibilities through a different lens. We share our successes with her, but we also share our missteps and our failures and how we manage them. She sees the whole picture, and she knows there's a solution to every problem.

Neither Gerald nor I grew up with examples of this kind of abundance in our families or in our neighborhoods, and yet, we were able to choose this path. We're creating a wealthy life in ways our primary influences, including our parents and grandparents, never saw as available to them. Reagan has a head start because we changed the narrative for ourselves, and by extension, for her. We hope these new ways of thinking will be passed on to her children and her children's children, growing stronger, more specific, and more fruitful with each generation. We've created a generational legacy that will serve our descendants well.

Deciding to live by the Six Pillars of Wealth and changing my narrative around money has resulted in a much different life than I would've otherwise had. I'm so much further along than the women and men who came before me were at my age. I'm so grateful for their sacrifices. I'm grateful for everything they did or experienced and everything they worked for because it all contributed to who I am today. But I also recognize I had to make a conscious choice to do some things differently. I had to learn from their successes and from their mistakes. I had to choose what to repeat, what to improve upon, and what to leave behind. I hope Reagan makes the same conscious choices and changes and improves upon the narrative I'm passing on to her.

Many of us come from challenging money stories, stories of not having enough, of trading hours for dollars, of constant hard work to create a sustainable lifestyle. However, that doesn't have to be the story you pass along to your children and grandchildren, nieces and nephews, or any of the young people who look to you to understand how the world works. Whether you grew up with plenty of money, your family scraped by, or you were solidly middle class, if you're not happy with the money narrative you grew up with, you can release it. You can replace it with a narrative of abundance and opportunity.

How things have always been for your family or your community in the past doesn't have to be how they always are. Acknowledge that it can be changed, and then do the work to make that change happen. Examine your blueprints and change those that no longer serve you. Challenge yourself to have a better relationship with money than any of your primary influences ever had. From life insurance to credit card debts to student loans and investing in the stock market, someone passed on their ideas to you, but you don't have to keep them. Seek evidence that any narrative holding you back isn't true, and act accordingly.

I grew up in a tiny apartment in South Central Los Angeles, in a gang-infested and crime-ridden neighborhood, but that wasn't the way it had to be for the rest of my life or for my child. Setting the intention to have a daily awareness in these pillars has transformed my life and taking similar action can transform yours too. You can have the wealthy life—as you define it—that you desire. Tell your story, share what you've experienced, and change the narrative for what can be.

### Redefine Wealth for Yourself

Commit to making the Six Pillars of Wealth a part of your daily life. Do the work to live a new narrative, and share it with the next generation, that they may do even better and learn early to redefine wealth for themselves.

For more resources to support your journey to Redefining Wealth visit:

RedefineWealthforYourself.com

# Acknowledgments

Writing this book was one of the most difficult tasks of my professional career. While this wasn't my first book and I certainly hope not my last, it required more out of me mentally, physically and emotionally than I realized when I began the task. It would have never manifested without the support of incredible people I must acknowledge.

Mom, my work ethic, compassion, stage presence and willingness to forgive comes from you. Your immeasurable sacrifice for me to be in this position is something I can never repay. I will never be able to fully articulate my appreciation.

Dad, you introduced me to the idea of entrepreneurship as a possibility in 3rd grade. Not sure I would've ever experienced this level of fulfillment had I not known this was an option so early on.

Gerald and Reagan, thank you for sharing me with the world. I know it's not easy to love someone so fiercely committed to their purpose, but you show me so much grace, support, love and encouragement and I'm grateful God chose us for one another.

Candice Davis, thank you for helping bring this to life. You were the first person I called when the idea dropped in my spirit. Unfortunately, that means you had to deal with all of my changes and indecisiveness too. You handled my antics with grace and true professionalism. I appreciate you.

To my business besties, acquaintances and mentors, over the years: Rushion McDonald, Dr. Dennis Kimbro, Lisa Nichols, Doreen Rainey, Lori and Chris Harder, Sheri Riley, Brandi Harvey, Rachel Luna, Marshawn Evans Daniels, Brooke Thomas, Ellie Kay, Cathy Heller, Stephen Hart, Donald Kelly, Tiffany Southerland and so many others. Thank you!

To my first grade teacher, Ms. Boynton, thank you for seeing my gift when no one else could.

To my team, people see Patrice Washington, but I see your tireless effort and belief that Redefining Wealth is greater than all of us. I couldn't do this without you!

# Endnotes

1   Harvard Health Publishing. 2019. "Writing about Emotions May Ease Stress and Trauma - Harvard Health." Harvard Health. Harvard Health. 2019. https://www.health.harvard.edu/healthbeat/writing-about-emotions-may-ease-stress-and-trauma.

2   "Learn About Mental Health - Mental Health - CDC." 2018. Centers for Disease Control and Prevention. 2018. https://www.cdc.gov/mentalhealth/learn/index.htm.

3   "The Best Grief Definition You Will Find." 2013. The Grief Recovery Method. 2013. https://www.griefrecoverymethod.com/blog/2013/06/best-grief-definition-you-will-find

4   Dalton, Tanya. 2019. *The Joy of Missing out: Live More by Doing Less*. Nashville, TN: Nelson Books, An Imprint of Thomas Nelson.

5   Inc, Pixie Technology. n.d. "Lost and Found: The Average American Spends 2.5 Days Each Year Looking for Lost Items Collectively Costing U.S. Households $2.7 Billion Annually in Replacement Costs." Www. Prnewswire.Com. Accessed October 11, 2020. https://www.prnewswire.com/news-releases/lost-and-found-the-average-american-spends-25-days-each-year-looking-for-lost-items-collectively-costing-us-households-27-billion-annually-in-replacement-costs-300449305.

6   Lee, Wendy. 2019. "People Spend More Time on Mobile Devices than TV, Firm Says." Los Angeles Times. Los Angeles Times. June 5, 2019. https://www.latimes.com/business/la-fi-ct-people-spend-more-time-on-mobile-than-tv-20190605-story.html.

7   Metev, Denis. 2019. "How Much Time Do People Spend on Social Media in 2020?" Review 42. September 3, 2019. https://review42.com/how-much-time-do-people-spend-on-social-media/.

8    "DAVINA BENNETT on Instagram: 'I Did Not Win but I Got What
     I Was Seeking. I Won the Hearts of Many, I Got to Highlight Deaf
     Awareness, I Stand as the First Afro Queen To....'" n.d. Instagram.
     Accessed October 11, 2020. https://www.instagram.com/p/
     Bb_-RdMAPC-/?utm_source=ig_web_copy_link.

9    American Psychological Association. 2012. "Building Your
     Resilience." *Https://Www.Apa.Org*, 2012. https://www.apa.org/topics/
     resilience.

10   Transformation Church. 2020. "In The Middle // Easter at
     Transformation Church 2020 (Michael Todd)." *YouTube*. https://www.
     youtube.com/watch?v=vHnzVaJg68o.

11   "Racial and Ethnic Disparities Continue in Pregnancy-Related Deaths."
     2019. Centers for Disease Control and Prevention. 2019. https://www.
     cdc.gov/media/releases/2019/p0905-racial-ethnic-disparities-
     pregnancy-deaths.html.

12   Gurchiek, Kathy, and Kathy Gurchiek. 2019. "Study: Women Negotiate
     Pay When Given the Chance." SHRM. May 10, 2019. https://www.shrm.
     org/hr-today/news/hr-news/pages/more-professionals-are-negotiating-
     salaries-than-in-the-past.aspx#:~:text=In%202018%2C%2068%20
     percent%20of.

13   Knueven, Liz. n.d. "The Average Monthly Mortgage Payment by State,
     City, and Year." Business Insider. Accessed October 11, 2020. https://
     www.businessinsider.com/personal-finance/average-mortgage-payment.

14   "The Fed - Dealing with Unexpected Expenses." n.d. Board of Governors
     of the Federal Reserve System. https://www.federalreserve.gov/publ
     ications/2019-economic-well-being-of-us-households-in-2018-deal
     ing-with-unexpected-expenses.htm.

15   Tatham, Matt. 2019. "Consumer Debt Reaches $13 Trillion in Q4 2018."
     Experian.Com. August 28, 2019. https://www.experian.com/blogs/
     ask-experian/research/consumer-debt-study/.